Euripides: Hippolytus

DUCKWORTH COMPANIONS
TO GREEK AND ROMAN TRAGEDY

Euripides: Hippolytus

Sophie Mills

Duckworth

This impression 2006
First published in 2002
Gerald Duckworth & Co. Ltd.
90-93 Cowcross Street, London EC1M 6BF
Tel: 020 7490 7300
Fax: 020 7490 0080
inquiries@duckworth-publishers.co.uk
www.ducknet.co.uk

A catalogue record for this book is available
from the British Library

ISBN 0 7156 2974 3
EAN 9780715629741

Contents

AEGEAN SEA

IONIAN SEA

Saronic
Gulf

Athens

Trozen

Sparta

1

Euripides and His World

Although many writers of tragedy lived and worked in Athens, the only full texts to have survived into the modern era are by the three acknowledged masters of the genre. This tragic trium-virate consists of Aeschylus (525-456 BC), Sophocles (496-406/5 BC) and Euripides. His play *Hippolytus* tells the story of Hip-polytus' punishment for disrespect to the goddess Aphrodite, and how that punishment is accomplished through the agency of his stepmother Phaedra and father Theseus, king of Athens and Trozen. The play has been generally acknowledged to be one of Euripides' finest, both for his skilled reworking of a traditional myth, and for the richness and complexity of its thought and language.

Euripides was born in Athens sometime between 485 and 480 (the tradition that he was born on the day of the naval battle of Salamis when the Athenians led the Greeks to a decisive victory over their Persian enemies seems too good to be true), and his life-span coincides almost exactly with the birth, rise and rela-tively swift decline of the empire of the Athenians that developed out of the anti-Persian alliance they led in the 480s and 470s BC. His youth was spent during the exciting early days of the alliance, but as he grew older, the allied cities felt increas-ing resentment towards a city that was beginning to treat them as mere subjects. When Euripides was over 50, in 431 BC, the long-simmering tensions arising from Athenian dominance in Greece triggered the Peloponnesian War, which divided most of Greece between partisans of Athens and of Sparta. The war was waged, on and off, until 404, when Sparta finally conquered Athens. Euripides died in 406, so did not live to see his city's defeat.

The imperial and economic power of Athens turned the city into a place of unparalleled culture and intellectual activity, and its reputation attracted many of the most exciting talents of the day, innovators in literature, art, science and philosophy. Euripides was strongly influenced by them, and as a result his tragedies are often highly intellectual in tone and full of questions on intellectual or moral issues of the day which he raises without offering any clear answers. His plays have recently held great appeal to the modern world, since some of the great issues of the late twentieth century – women's rights, civil rights, the morality of war, the relative influences of nature versus nurture, even the value of the literary canon full of 'dead white European males' such as Euripides – all have their counterparts in the issues raised by this most modern of the three tragedians. Euripides' plays are shaped by fifth-century 'cutting-edge' speculations on the value of war and other traditional Greek pursuits, on the nature of the gods, and on the distinctions between slave and free, male and female, Greek and barbarian that shaped Greek thought.

An ancient biographical tradition about Euripides exists, but its reliability can be judged from its assertion that the inspiration for his *Hippolytus* was his second wife's infidelity. Like all such biography, it relies heavily on anecdotes and on the assumption that a poet's writings literally reflect his life. Some of the tradition may ultimately derive from contemporary perceptions of Euripides: the claims that he was a recluse who wrote his plays in a cave on Salamis are suspiciously picturesque, but the consistency of his characterisation as a quiet, rather gloomy man may indicate that he was not as outgoing as his contemporary Sophocles.[1] On the whole, however, the biographical tradition is probably best left alone, and we may turn our attention instead to what is known of his dramatic output. Ascribed to Euripides are 92 plays, of which 19 have come down to the modern world. Greek tragedies were performed in an annual competition between three playwrights chosen by the state, who presented four plays at a time to the Athenian public. From inscriptions listing the prize-winners, we learn that in 31 competitions, Sophocles won first prize 18 times, otherwise always coming second. By contrast, in 22 competitions, Euripidean plays took a mere 5 first prizes, one of which was for the set of tragedies that included *Hippolytus*. While it would be wrong to conclude from these statistics, as many later writers of antiquity did, that the Athenians hated Euripides – if they had, he would not have been able to present his plays at public expense year after year[2] – they apparently found it harder to give him the unqualified admiration that they offered to his contemporary Sophocles or his predecessor Aeschylus, whose work acquired classic status almost immediately after his death.

Our best, if biased, witness for contemporary attitudes to Euripides is Aristophanes, a writer of comedy some years his junior, who fills his comedies with quotations or parodies of Euripidean tragedy, and even writes Euripides himself as a character into some of his comedies. The genre in which Aristophanes was writing ('Old Comedy') typically views society in a mocking and frequently 'conservative' light. Intellectuals are a favourite source of Aristophanic humour, and his characters skewer those who waste time in speculations guaranteed to be either fruitless or immoral on topics concerning which all right-thinking people know the answer. (I should add that this is not Aristophanes' only persona, for he is also an acute judge of poetry and critic of such conservatives as well: his essential aim is to make his audience laugh, by whatever means he can find.) Partly for comic effect, and perhaps partly for more serious ends, Aristophanes portrays Euripides as a ridiculous intellectual whose output is pretentious, senseless or immoral. Yet his very ubiquity in Aristophanes indicates his importance in the literary landscape of Athens.

In Aristophanes' comedy *The Frogs*, which was presented soon after Euripides' death, Dionysus descends to the underworld in order to resurrect either Euripides or Aeschylus, to help Athens in a time of crisis during the Peloponnesian War. In a contest between the two, each shows off his own merits and tries to decry the other. Aeschylus represents traditional Athenian moral and literary values, while Euripides is a modernist. Aeschylus criticises Euripides for writing high-flown twaddle, for creating low-born characters who have no business in the elevated genre of tragedy, and most importantly, for making his characters, especially his women, engage in rhetorically sophisticated, but dangerously immoral justifications of incest, bestiality, infanticide and other typical elements of Greek myth. He says that some of Euripides' subjects are simply unfit for decent society – a complaint familiar to avant-garde artists of every age. More than Sophocles or Aeschylus, Euripides does like topics which provide shock-value: notoriously in his *Aeolus*, the incest taboo is claimed to be a mere matter of convention, in the *Medea*, the sun-god lends an infanticidal mother his chariot so that she can escape from her crime, while he devotes two plays to the incestuous and adulterous love of Phaedra for her stepson Hippolytus. This is, of course, not to deny that many aspects of Euripidean tragedy are highly traditional: the plot of the *Hippolytus* in which a spurned goddess punishes disrespect has many parallels in Greek literature, and, like those of Sophocles and Aeschylus, his themes derive from a body of mythology that had existed for centuries. Even so, certain differences in tone and focus between Euripidean tragedy and the work of the other two tragedians are quite clear.

The essence of tragedy is that someone does something wrong, often because of his limited human perception, and is punished terribly by the gods. As Aristotle says in his *Poetics*, the tragic hero can therefore neither be a completely good man (for then his punishment would seem unfair) nor a completely bad one (for then it would be just). A tragic hero must also be both recognisable as a human being to his audience so that they can identify with him, but remain a little distanced from them so that they can watch and analyse the cause of his sufferings with a measure of detachment. One of Euripides' particular trademarks is the grafting of realism onto the old myths so that his heroes are more like ordinary people than the slightly remote and not always realistic figures of Aeschylus. Aristotle quotes Sophocles as saying that he himself portrayed people as they ought to be, but Euripides, as they actually are. Euripides undoubtedly has a particular interest in individual psychology for its own sake.

Just as Euripides' heroes are less elevated than those of his dramatic contemporaries, so Euripidean drama gives especial prominence to women, slaves and sometimes non-Greeks. The unusually important role that the Nurse plays in the *Hippolytus* is indicative of this tendency. Greek thought laid great emphasis on the divisions between free and slave, Greek and barbarian, man and beast, male and female, privileging the former at the latter's expense. Euripides often works against traditional ideas and expectations of tragedy, both by concentrating more on those to whom it had not given particular prominence, and by his interests in realism and in individual psychology. Although its dramatic structure is highly traditional, the *Hippolytus* is an excellent example of Euripides' fondness for defying audience expectations, as I will show in subsequent chapters.

In order to understand Euripides' portrayal of Phaedra in the *Hippolytus*, it is essential to keep in mind Greek stereotypes of women and their role in Athenian culture.[3] Strong, menacing women had long been major figures in Greek myth, and there is clearly common ground between Euripides' dangerous women and those such as Circe in the *Odyssey* who try to harm Odysseus. Women were often conceptualised in Greek thought as essentially destructive of male society by means of their powerful sexuality. Homer's Helen and Clytemnestra are 'typical': only Penelope is a counter-example, and she is exceptional. A little later in Greek thought, Hesiod characterises women as not only dangerous – the first woman, Pandora, opens her box out of curiosity and causes all the troubles in the world – but also as a drain on men's resources: they stay at home in comfort while the men toil outside.[4] The seventh-century satirist Semonides takes the further step of assimilating women to different animals: the virtuous Bee Woman avoids the sexual talk of the other women and concentrates instead on building her husband's wealth (Semonides 7.84-94), but all the others, such as the Pig Woman (7.1-6) or the Monkey Woman (7.70-83), are dirty or lazy or greedy or annoying or untrustworthy or some combination of these attributes.

Hippolytus himself is one of the many Greek males who fantasise about a world without women (*Hippolytus* 616ff.), and Athens' own patron goddess Athena was supposed to have avoided the taint of femininity by emerging from the head of her father Zeus. Yet in reality, the male line cannot be reproduced without a woman, and hence men are ambivalent towards them. A woman is necessary to carry on men's families, but since she comes from another family, her loyalties must always be suspect. Therefore she must be kept away from outside influences, but then she becomes Hesiod's kept woman who wastes the resources that the man must provide. Since he cannot supervise her constantly, he is always afraid that she is deceiving him, whether by enjoying more food and drink than is her due, or even by sneaking a lover into the house and having a child with him, thereby polluting his family line. Moreover, women bleed and give birth, so that they are aligned with the irrational forces of nature that must be tamed and contained as much as possible. The physical weakness of women as compared to men is translated into a moral weakness, so that women are held to be lacking in self-control, and excessively prone to physical desire and emotionalism. To lack self-control is to be enslaved to one's passions, and thus to be less than truly free: in a slave-owning society the distinction between slave and free is vital.[5] Moreover, any society like Athens which connects the privileges of citizenship with military service on its behalf will make women politically weak, so that perceptions of women's innate mental and physical limitations 'naturally' lead to the imposition of limitations on women, which in their turn help to 'prove' female inferiority.

Unflattering images of women are hardly confined to Greek culture, but a strong strain of misogyny runs through Greek literature from earliest times, and certain socio-cultural factors peculiar to fifth-century Athens seem to give myths of danger-ous women a particular resonance in a city where there is evidence that women had fewer freedoms than in some other parts of Greece. Paradoxically, the change from aristocratic government to democracy during the sixth and fifth centuries at Athens seems to have liberated Athenian males while dimin-ishing women's freedoms, in that political power confined to a very few aristocratic males created fewer divisions between male and female roles than a society in which all males, but no females, participated in the democratic assembly.[6] In fifth-century Athens, every woman was under the control of a *kurios* – literally 'one who has power' – a male relative who was her legal representative and had considerable influence on matters such as whom she should marry and the management of her prop-erty. Many texts prescribe that a woman should stay at home with her children and look after the house, and that she should ideally be 'least mentioned for praise or blame'.[7] Only for relig-ious purposes (which would probably include the dramatic festivals in Athens),[8] was a female public presence acceptable. Recent scholarship[9] offers a more nuanced view of women in Athens, allowing for differences between ages and socio-economic classes – for example, the ideal of seclusion would not have been a practical reality for poorer women who would need to fetch water from the fountain for the day's needs, or even to work in the market or the fields – but the very clear divisions between men and women and certain difficulties arising therefrom cannot be ignored.

Since our era has been influenced so profoundly by feminism, we tend to assume that women living under this apparently oppressive regime must keenly have resented it, although what seems appalling to us now would have seemed less so even 100 years ago, when women were equally debarred from many areas of public life. That so much extant Greek drama concerns destructive or destroyed women would suggest that some anxieties and inequalities existed and were acknowledged. If questions arising from the differences between the treatment of men and women in a society that prided itself on the equality between citizens were part of current speculation among intellectuals, Euripides could have incorporated these into his plays, as he does with other topics arising from advanced discourse in fifth-century Athens. Greek tragedy and comedy can both function as a kind of public safety valve for acknowledging social discontents, so that they did not fester and damage society, while the Greek myths that the tragedians dramatised often explain why certain conditions of human life are as they are. Thus when Euripides uses a Phaedra or a Medea to portray female frustrations, but also shows the terrible actions that they take to transcend their social limitations, he simultaneously expresses an awareness of inequalities between men and women, while ultimately endorsing the status quo and explaining why women cannot have male freedoms.

It would, however, be wrong to read Euripides' plays about

women as anything resembling the first dawning of a feminist consciousness. At most, such plays are questioning traditional practices rather than advocating a change in society that only appeared over 2000 years after Euripides' day. Though oppressive by our standards, a woman's role in charge of the day-to-day running of the house could have been fulfilling, even in a cultural context in which the superiority of the male in public life is essentially taken for granted. Nonetheless, the limitations imposed on women arising from negative stereotypes are an essential background to understanding Phaedra in the *Hippolytus*.

The Athenians found Euripides' work difficult because it raised complex questions to which there were no easy answers. Similarly inconclusive, yet stimulating as thinkers, are the philosophers and teachers of rhetoric known as the sophists, with whom Euripides was closely associated in the minds of his contemporaries.[10] Our sources for sophistic thought, especially Plato, are hostile to them, and mere fragments of their actual works survive, but they were a dynamic intellectual presence in fifth-century Athens. Men such as Protagoras, Prodicus, Hippias and others offered a kind of higher education, for which they were well paid by young men who were often well-off and politically ambitious. Different individuals had their special areas of expertise, but all of them claimed to teach *aretê*, which can mean moral excellence or virtue, but also all the qualities necessary for success in public life and especially the political life of the Athenian democracy, in which an intelligent man with a persuasive tongue could gain prestige and influence among his contemporaries. Typical of sophistic teaching is a deep interest in language, and especially in the nature of the relationship between words, thoughts and objects. Hence they tend to speculate on the relationships between the world and the senses, truth and perception, appearance and reality, between what is natural (*phusis*) and what is merely a matter of conven-

15

tion (*nomos*), the existence of the gods and the nature of justice (does either objectively exist or is belief in them mere convention?) and in the power of language to influence human perception. The popularity of the sophists in Athens may be attributed to their fascination with argument, since rhetorical expertise was essential for anyone who wished to make a name for himself in the assembly or law-courts that were so important in the democracy.

Sophistic styles of thought quickly lead to relativism and scepticism concerning 'truths' that had previously been accepted without question, and the relativist Protagoras is an especially important figure among the sophists. He is credited with the statement, 'Man is the measure of all things', and with the claim that about everything, there are two possible arguments – the stronger and the weaker – and that it is always possible to turn one into the other. While in origin this statement is surely connected with his doctrine that no man's perception could be actually false, but only more or less persuasive, it is a short gap to interpret 'stronger' and 'weaker' as 'better' and 'worse', and thus to argue that moral is immoral and vice versa. The power of language is always ambiguous, since a skilled persuader can easily become a skilled liar. It is obvious that anyone interested in questioning such fundamentals as the relationship between appearance and reality and the relationship between morality, nature and convention might easily be accused of deliberately seeking to undermine right conduct, hence the sophists had their share of detractors. Moreover, since they claimed that they could teach anyone *aretê*, they made a threateningly democratic challenge to traditional claims that 'virtue' was innate and unteachable. Sophistic argument is also often couched in terms of a contest, whereby winning through clever arguments becomes more important than the search for truth – Euripidean tragedy is full of rhetorically sophisticated pairs of speeches in opposition to one another – and with some

16

justification, Plato complains that their method of argument is merely for show rather than an attempt to find the truth. The Nurse in the *Hippolytus* is a particularly good example of the dangers of sophistic thought at its worst.

The accusations of immorality and disgraceful speculation that dogged the sophists are precisely those levelled at Euripides by 'Aeschylus' in Aristophanes' *Frogs*. Euripides was said to have known Protagoras personally and to have been involved in the circles in which the scientist Anaxagoras and Pericles were also members. Advanced intellectual ideas pervade Euripidean drama, and his plays are full of sophistic rhetoric, as well as speculations derived from the most up-to-date theories of the natural philosophers who shared with the sophists a view of the world which explained natural phenomena in a mechanistic, rather than a theological manner. Thus later sources allege that the motivation of his visit to the court of Archelaus, king of Macedon, in 408 BC was to escape Athenian hostility to such ideas, but in fact it was quite normal for poets to be hired by kings who wanted to raise the cultural prestige of their courts. Aeschylus had accepted a similar invitation from Sicily some 50 years previously. It would appear that Euripides died in 406, while still abroad, although the story that he was torn to pieces by dogs certainly derives from the plot of his own play the *Bacchae* and may be ignored.

At the time of the production of the *Hippolytus* in 428, when the Peloponnesian War had been going on for three years, Euripides had been competing for nearly 30 years, and it appears that he had already dramatised one version of the Hippolytus story which had become notorious for its explicit portrayal of Phaedra's desire for her stepson. Since certain myths had huge dramatic possibilities that could not be exhausted by even several treatments, it was quite normal for playwrights to use myths that their colleagues had already used. Three different versions of the story of Electra by the three playwrights are still extant, Sophocles revisited the myths of Oedipus throughout his life and we know that playwrights would sometimes rewrite parts of previously produced plays. However, as far as we know, Euripides is unique in his treatment of the Hippolytus myth for taking exactly the same story and presenting two entirely different versions of it to the Athenian public.

2

Tragedy and the Hippolytus Story

Tragedy and Athens

By the time Euripides wrote the *Hippolytus*, tragedy was a
mature art form that had been part of Athenian cultural life for
over a century. The play was presented in 428 BC at the Great
Dionysia, a dramatic festival in which literature, artistic spec-
tacle, religion, politics and education all played a part. It took
place in mid- to late March and included worship of Dionysus,
processions and sacrifices as well as artistic performance. In its
heyday, the artistic part of the festival lasted five days: three of
these were devoted to tragedy, and on each of them, one writer
would present three tragedies and one satyr play.[1]

In organisation, the Dionysia straddled private and public
and professional and amateur, so as to blur the divisions between them and make it truly a festival of the whole Athenian
people. The actors were professionals, but the choruses were
ordinary male citizens, and while the chief magistrate of Athens
was in charge of its organisation, financing was divided between
the state and individuals. From the mid-fifth century onwards,
the state paid the actors and for an honorarium for the poets,
while wealthy individuals (*chorêgoi*)[2] volunteered to finance the
training of choruses, an act of generosity which would win them
credit among the Athenian people. One member from each of
the ten Athenian tribes was selected to sit on the board of judges
awarding prizes to the productions.[3]

The close connection of tragedy with Athenian public and political life is particularly indicated by certain preliminaries to the performances. Before they began, the ten generals of Athens poured libations to 'democracy, peace and good fortune', while the youths whose fathers had died fighting for the city, and who had therefore been brought up at the state's expense, marched in glory to their seats. Lists of honours conferred on those who had done service to the city were also read aloud. In the fifth century, the tribute collected from imperial Athens' subjects was even paraded before the audience.[4] Such preliminaries created a sense of unity and pride in the city's achievements among the Athenians in the audience, and may have disposed them to be especially receptive to the educative function that is so important in Greek tragedy.

The performance of tragedy

Records for tragic productions only trace them back securely to 501 BC, but doubtless the form had been evolving for some time previously. In his *Poetics*, chapter 4, Aristotle states that tragedy originated when the 'leaders of the dithyramb' became soloists engaging in dialogue with the chorus. His claim that choral poetry lies behind tragedy is consistent with the fact that a second actor was not introduced until Aeschylus, while the chorus is usually on stage throughout nearly the entire drama, far longer than any one actor. Even in Euripides' day, only three speaking actors ever performed on stage at any one time. Since the number of individual characters in tragedies always exceeds three, the actors must take several parts each, an arrangement which seems to exclude the possibility of method acting or especially close identification between actor and character played. Vase paintings show that the (male) actors wore masks, long embroidered robes with sleeves and high boots.

The constant presence of the chorus – 15 by Euripides' day –

on stage shows that they are an essential element of tragedy. They are often characterised as citizens or – as in the *Hippolytus* – attendants of one of the leading characters. They have their own perspective on the action, but, unlike the actors, chorus members are not the moral agents of the play whose choices create the action. In most extant drama, the individual actors are central in interest, and the chorus do not act as much as react to the actors' adventures and sufferings, in the choral songs that alternate with the episodes of the action. The demands of an increasing realism in Euripides can even make their ubiquity somewhat inconvenient: in the *Hippolytus*, the chorus have observed Phaedra continuously on stage and know that her accusation is false, but they can only hint at this to Theseus, because Euripides has had to make them swear an oath of silence to her, in order to have a plausible explanation of why they simply do not tell him the truth.

Euripides' *Hippolytus* was performed in the Theatre of Dionysus, just above the temple of Dionysus on the hillside south-east of the Acropolis. Substantial remains of a theatre are visible today, but these are of a later date. The ancient theatre consisted of an area called the *orchêstra* ('dancing-place') which is associated with choral song and dance. Later theatres had a separate raised stage for the actors, but this may be a post-Euripidean development. Behind the orchestra was a wooden building called the *skênê*, 12 metres long and 4 high, which had a flat roof (*theologeion*) on which divine appearances on high could be made, a door in the middle and, at least for later plays, a backdrop extending from it on either side. This façade was both a piece of scenery that could be painted to denote a particular setting, and a sounding board to help the acoustics in the theatre. The building itself doubled both as a changing room for the actors and as any structure which they entered, such as a palace or even a cave. Two paths (*parodoi* or *eisodoi*) on either side led off the stage and served as roads to and from the city in

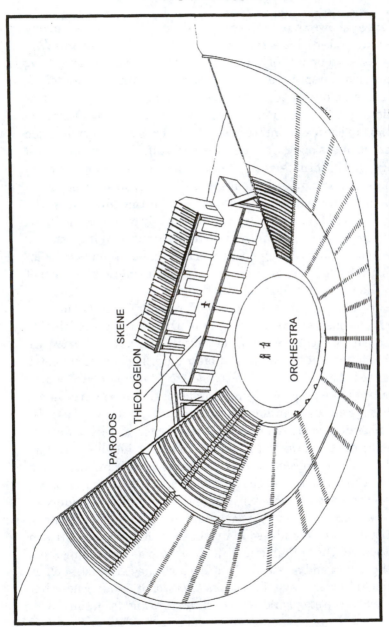

Elevation of a Greek theatre. Adapted from a drawing by E.R. Malyon, from E. Csapo and W. Slater, *The Context of Ancient Drama* (Ann Arbor: University of Michigan Press).

SKENE

PARODOS

THEOLOGEION

ORCHESTRA

which the drama was set. One of the conventions that seems most odd to those used to proscenium theatres in which the spectator is a kind of spy looking into a room, is that the action of a Greek tragedy is always performed outside. When indoor scenes or tableaux – often of dead bodies – are necessary, realism is suspended and a wheeled wooden platform, the *ek-kyklêma*, is rolled out of the *skênê* building to allow the audience to 'enter' the palace briefly and view the picture within.

Simple practicality dictates this and other conventions of the Greek tragic stage. The theatre of Dionysus held an audience of maybe 12,000-14,000 people seated around three-quarters of the orchestra, and it would be impossible for most of them to see or hear action that took place within the *skênê* building. The view at the back of the theatre, some 200 feet above the orchestra, would be restricted, and it is generally thought that the acoustics were reasonably good, but not as good as those, for example, in the later theatre at Epidaurus where dramatic performances are held to this day. Sight and sound were also aided by the masks worn by the actors, which both emphasised their faces – subtlety of expression is pointless in a huge arena – and may have helped to augment their natural voices. The use of masks also helps to broaden the reference of the action, to suggest that what is happening is not only a particular occurrence, but is emblematic of particular types of human existence. For reasons of practicality and religious propriety, violent action is never portrayed on stage, but a messenger reports what has happened: as in radio drama, imagination is more effective than literal representation. Just as the performers must act with large gestures in order to be visible in a large public place, so it is the large themes of human existence that they tend to explore, and there is little place for the subtleties or individual psychological quirks that are important in our theatre. Although Euripidean tragedy has a greater tendency towards realistic characterisation than some earlier tragedies, Greek tragedy is neither as realistic nor as intimate as much of our theatre.

A typical structure for a tragedy – though there are many variants – is the following: a prologue in monologue or dialogue form by the actors, which establishes the details necessary for the audience to understand what is coming, followed by a song (*parodos*) sung by the chorus as they enter the stage. Then the plot gradually unfolds as the actors interact with one another in longer speeches and dialogue. These 'episodes' are separated from one another by songs (*stasima*) sung and danced by the chorus to a musical accompaniment of wind instruments. The part of the play following the last stasimon is the *exodos*, at the end of which the chorus makes its exodus from the stage. Though it is often obscured in modern translation and performance, tragedy is poetry, and there is a strong correlation between the type of poetry used and the type of tragic discourse presented. Iambic trimeter, the metre closest to normal speech rhythms, was the standard metre for actors' speech.[5] Various kinds of interaction in this metre were possible between actors, ranging from monologues through extended dialogue to *stichomythia* ('speaking in lines') in which actors speak alternating lines in a kind of stylised conversation. The *agôn*, or contest, pits two characters against one another: one gives a speech about an issue central to the tragedy, and the other attempts a refutation through a second monologue, followed by dialogue between them. Such speeches are common in Euripides and are particularly influenced by contemporary forensic oratory, and the sophistic rhetoric discussed in Chapter 1.

The chorus can converse with the actors in iambic trimeter, but their discourse is commonly carried out in various sung lyric metres: particular metres are associated with different levels of emotional intensity. Actors can also communicate with the chorus in lyric metres. The language of the choral odes is quite different from that of the episodes: it is generalised, and often obscure, with emphasis on poetic imagery and leaps in time and place. By contrast, the language of the actors is more influenced by rhetoric and logic – the chorus, as it were, sings 'right-brained' poetry versus the 'left-brained' poetry of the actors. Their perspective and style open the play up beyond linear narrative. They are not bound by time, so can move from present to past to future, in order to link the play with wider themes in myth or human experience. While the chorus often have a collective identity as citizens or attendants, and can sometimes represent 'the common man', choral identity is not consistent, and the tragedians tend to use the chorus to high-light whatever aspects of the action they want at a particular moment. The fluidity of their status forbids neat classifications of their role, just as their lyric ranges beyond the here and now of the dramatic action.

Aristotle (*Poetics* 6.2-3) defines tragedy as an imitation of an action that is 'serious, complete and of a certain size', and tragedy nearly always dramatises myths about the big themes of human existence, such as the family, the role of women, the role of the individual in society and the relationship of men to gods, all of which are themes in the *Hippolytus*. Hippolytus himself, and arguably Phaedra, could justly be described in Aristotle's terms as someone 'not pre-eminent in virtue and justice, and one who falls into affliction not because of evil and wickedness but because of a certain fallibility'.[6] The hero's suffering instils 'pity and terror' in the audience, and this is achieved by dealings between 'those who are bonded by kinship or friendship', particularly when one harms another in igno-rance, and later discovers the truth, as happens when Theseus curses Hippolytus. Often – as in the *Hippolytus* – the destroyed hero destroys other members of his family with him. Such plots have many layers and themes and are therefore amenable to more than one interpretation, and though Hippolytus' circumstances are not literally like those of anyone in the audience, he is recognisable as a human being with recognisable failings from which he incurs a suffering which is excessive but comprehensible to the audience. Thus the minds of the audience are educated and their emotions are given release.

The Hippolytus myth before Euripides

Only one of the two plays on the Hippolytus theme composed by Euripides survives. Some 25 short fragments of the lost play remain, along with a similar number from a play by Sophocles called *Phaedra*, which dramatised the same topic. Before discussing what is known of the lost plays and how they probably differed from the extant play, it is helpful to summarise the mythological tradition concerning Hippolytus and Phaedra that Euripides would have inherited.

Though the location of the Hippolytus myth varies between Athens or Trozen in the north-east Peloponnese, all sources agree that Theseus' second wife Phaedra fell in love with her stepson Hippolytus and tried to seduce him. When he repudiated her, she falsely accused him of rape. His father Theseus believed her accusation and asked his divine father Poseidon to curse Hippolytus. Poseidon did his son's bidding by sending a bull from the sea to terrify Hippolytus' horses, so that they threw him off his chariot, injuring him fatally, and the truth was revealed when it was too late to make amends. At some point in the story, Phaedra hanged herself. Phaedra's only role in Greek myth is to fall in love with Hippolytus, so that I assume that any mention of her implies knowledge of the Hippolytus story. If so, it can be traced back to the sixth century BC and may be even older. One early epic mentions Theseus' two marriages, one to an Amazon (Hippolytus' mother) and one to Phaedra. Homer also mentions Phaedra along with her sister Ariadne, who was also unhappily involved with Theseus (*Odyssey* 11.321f.) The sixth-century epic *Naupaktika* refers to Hippolytus' subsequent resurrection by the god Asclepius, which is taken up by Virgil and others (see Chapter 6). The version of the story which rewards his death with a cult has, however, a logical consistency and is likely to be the earlier story.

Since no other narrative is known concerning the three, and the Hippolytus story is not closely connected with the extensive traditions surrounding Theseus as king of Attica, it is probable that the story originates in Trozen, and that the Athenian location is a later development, especially since Hippolytus is only a minor hero at Athens, while at Trozen he was important enough to command a large precinct, a priest and annual sacrifices (Pausanias, *Description of Greece* 2.32.1). In spite of the hatred of Aphrodite that Euripides ascribes to Hippolytus, he seems to have had a much stronger connection in cult with her than with Artemis. Both at Athens and at Trozen, his precinct contained a temple of Aphrodite, and in Trozenian cult he was worshipped by unmarried girls, as both Euripides' plays mention. His cult may therefore originally have been connected with young girls' rites of passage from virginity to marriage, and his myth, like some others, may have contained an implied warning to young women about the dire consequences of refusing marriage.

The fragmentary Hippolytus plays

About 300 tragedies by the three great tragedians were originally extant: barely one tenth of these survived into the middle ages, due to the vagaries of textual transmission in the ancient world. Around AD 200, ten tragedies of Euripides were somehow selected – by whom is unknown – as the best of his work, and from then on, it was these that were read and copied, while the others were gradually read less and less until eventually they were lost, which was the fate of the other *Hippolytus* and Sophocles' *Phaedra*.

There is no hope of reconstructing a lost play, but often enough direct or indirect evidence survives for scholars to be able to make reasonable conjectures on some of its contents. Sometimes actual quotations are preserved, either on papyrus fragments or embedded in later writers quoting them for their own purposes. Then there are more general references to the play by writers summarising its plot or referring to some aspect of it. Lastly, one can sometimes guess at the content of a lost tragedy by looking at a later writer who has incorporated certain aspects of it into his own work. There are problems with all of these methods of conjecture. Fragments are often quoted either to show an example of unusual vocabulary, or by anthologists excerpting quotations on certain subjects, so that little about what happened in the tragedy can be gleaned from them. Later writers summarising plots tend to use more than one source, so that we cannot be sure what they are taking from a specific play. Again, the assumption that a later writer borrowed from a lost play might be very likely, but it is usually impossible to distinguish between borrowed elements and authorial innovations. Although none of these methods is unproblematic, these sources are all we have, since the hope of finding a whole manuscript of one of the lost plays is slender.

There is a division in later accounts of the *Hippolytus* story between those whose main source is the extant *Hippolytus*, and those whose account is so different that one of the lost tragedies is likely to be their literary model. In particular, the Hippolytus and Phaedra stories written by the Roman writers Ovid and Seneca (see Chapter 6) contrast with Euripides' version in portraying a woman who, unlike our Phaedra, gives her passion full rein. Fragments and other citations of the lost *Hippolytus* strongly suggest that its Phaedra was similarly uninhibited in her advances to Hippolytus. The first *Hippolytus* is distinguished from the second by the title *Hippolytus Kalyptomenos*, or 'Hippolytus Hiding Himself', and it is thought that the name derives from Hippolytus' gesture of hiding his head in horror as Phaedra propositioned him on stage. Aristophanes (*Frogs* 1043, 1052-3) cites Phaedra as a particularly shocking example of the outrageous females with whom Euripides is polluting the stage. Since the Phaedra of our extant play struggles valiantly to suppress her love, Aristophanes must surely refer to Phaedra in the lost play. It is therefore very likely that the Roman Phaedra is at least partly modelled on the Phaedra of Euripides' lost play. More than that, however, it is hard to state definitely, since we cannot assume that everything in Ovid and Seneca derives from Euripides or that they were incapable of innovation. Her very outrageousness would naturally encourage the Romans to put their own stamp on her wicked behaviour. Seneca's play has little in common with Euripides', apart from lines 360ff. which clearly recall *Hippolytus* 183-222 but do not fit well into their context. It is therefore likely enough that Seneca's basic framework recalls the lost play, even if it occasionally incorporates a little of the extant play, although just how closely Seneca and the first play corresponded to one another must remain uncertain.

Aristophanes of Byzantium, who edited the text of Euripides around 200 BC, says in his introductory summary of the extant *Hippolytus* that the lost play was condemned for its 'unseemly material', and that the second play was an attempt to make amends with the Athenian public. This motivation, as will be argued later, is unlikely, but he is probably right about the chronology of the two plays,[7] since the essential plot of the story is a recurrent motif in Greek and other mythologies, according to which a young man rejects the advances of an older woman. That he is her stepson adds an extra frisson in the *Hippolytus*. The story typically condemns the woman and supports the young man. It would seem logical that a play which meets audience expectations – evil woman, noble youth – should precede one which makes great efforts to undercut such expectations, and offers an unexpected defence for the 'obviously' bad Phaedra, while making judgements on Hippolytus' wisdom and virtue more complex. Such themes still lurk in modern popular culture, sometimes with the same colouring that condemns the woman and views the young man as a victim. Stories of older women seducing younger men are pure tabloid material, while the predatory older woman appears as Mrs Robinson in *The Graduate* – indeed, Benjamin Braddock rejects her advances with Hippolytean horror at first, though he is more easily worn down than his Greek predecessor. Phaedra's false charge of rape has many resonances in modern-day anxiety about sexual harassment and false accusations, both in real life and in films such as *Disclosure*.

The extant *Hippolytus* is significantly different from the version that is presumed to reflect the other play, but two plays, both called *Hippolytus*, must have had a number of common elements. As a minimum, the lost play must have included a scene revealing Phaedra's love for her stepson; a scene where he finds out and threatens to reveal all to his father; Phaedra's false accusation of rape; Theseus' condemnation of his son; the fulfilment of the curse by Poseidon's bull from the sea, and a final revelation of the truth and a prophecy that Hippolytus will be remembered in cult in Athens. Other elements are a matter of conjecture. One might guess that apart from the common details of *what* happened, Euripides gave very different accounts of *why* and *how* it happened in the two plays.

Many of the fragments are quoted to show how uninhibited Phaedra was in her advances to her stepson. 'I have love as a teacher in daring and boldness' (fr. 430)[8] is typical, and it would be interesting to know how far the first Phaedra shared the lax moral attitude of the Nurse in the extant play. The second Phaedra struggles desperately to restrain herself, even to the extent of starving herself to death rather than revealing her feelings to Hippolytus, but to no avail, since her love is Aphrodite's weapon against Hippolytus. The strong influence of divinity in the second play therefore helps to diminish her direct responsibility for her feelings towards her stepson. Fragment 444 of the lost play, 'O gods, how there is no escape for mortals from innate and god-sent evils', indicates that Phaedra's love in the first play must also have been divinely motivated, and in Seneca (*Phaedra* 124ff.), Phaedra's love is caused by Aphrodite's desire for revenge on all descendants of the Sun god, who once spied on her adulterous affair with Ares. The first Phaedra's reputation as an unscrupulous woman who lusted after an innocent young man is so consistent, however, that even if the cause of her love was ultimately attributed to a divinity in the lost play, it would appear that she was held responsible for her actions to a much greater extent than is the Phaedra of the extant play.

Persistent in later tradition is a suggestion by Phaedra to Hippolytus that he should take power in Theseus' absence: fragment 434 ('Men's fortunes do not always accord with their piety: by daring and violence everything is caught and hunted down') may be part of her invitation to Hippolytus to usurp his father.[9] At any rate, her proposal and its rejection must have been followed by the false accusation to Theseus: fragment 429, 'we women give birth to another fire in place of a fire, and one much harder to fight with', looks as though it comes just before such an accusation. Fragment 435 refers to the swearing of an oath, perhaps imposed on Hippolytus by Phaedra, not to tell Theseus what had happened. Again, the second *Hippolytus* deviates from this, since the accusation is made by letter rather than directly, and Phaedra kills herself before it is found, so that she cannot be cross-examined by anyone. Usually, she kills herself only after the truth is revealed, so that she can accuse Hippolytus directly to Theseus, who condemns his son without

further investigation. This detail may shed some light on Theseus' presentation in the earlier play: a man who trusts a
woman such as this Phaedra is perhaps less sympathetic than
a man who comes home to find his beloved and hitherto virtuous
wife dead by her own hand, bearing a letter accusing his son of
raping her. It would appear from fragment 440, 'Theseus, I give
you excellent advice, if you are sensible; do not trust a woman
even when you hear the truth', that he was explicitly advised to
retract his condemnation of Hippolytus.

With the exception of the extant *Hippolytus*, tradition places
Phaedra's love for Hippolytus at a time when Theseus was away
in Hades, helping his friend Peirithous to abduct the queen of
the underworld. In the surviving play, he is on a visit to an
unspecified oracle. We are never told why he has gone there, and
this not particularly well-motivated explanation would suggest
that Euripides was working against the usual tradition. In
early sources, Peirithous' abduction attempt is linked with
Theseus' abduction of the young Helen (of later Trojan fame):
the two friends made a pact to help one another secure daugh-
ters of Zeus as trophy wives. Plutarch (*Moralia* 27f-28a) says
that the first Phaedra attempted to excuse her love for Hippolytus by citing Theseus' own adulteries. Traditions of this
kind would have provided ample ammunition for her, and while
such attempts at self-justification would have made her even
more scandalous in Athenian eyes, her accusations would not
be flattering to Theseus either.

Early accounts of Theseus' visit to the underworld portrayed
it as an impious act for which he and Peirithous were punished
by eternal imprisonment below. When, from the mid-sixth century onwards, the Athenians promoted Theseus as their
national hero and symbol, they were faced with a somewhat
flawed character – though he was famous as the killer of the
Minotaur, it was embarrassing that he had then abandoned
Ariadne, and that he had been detained in the underworld in

this way. Thus the Athenians created new versions of the old, unflattering stories which transformed the journey to the underworld into a story about outstanding loyalty to a friend that motivated him to accompany him even unto death. Euripides' first play may have denied this attractive story. If the adventure in the underworld had been used to his discredit in the first *Hippolytus*, his absence in the second play removes him from all impropriety, while his devotion to Phaedra is also emphasised. Thus Theseus, as well as Phaedra, may have been 'cleaned up' in the second play.

Tradition is consistent that Theseus kills his son by invoking the aid of his divine father Poseidon. Poseidon had given his son three wishes as a mark of his favour, to be used as Theseus needed. In the first *Hippolytus* Theseus cursed his son with the third of these, and therefore must have known that the curse would take effect. By contrast, the second *Hippolytus* makes it clear that he is using the first of the wishes, and is apparently not sure that it will work. The effect is the same, but Theseus is more actively blameworthy in the earlier play than in this one. Fragment 442 refers to the bull from the sea, and we may assume that, as in the extant play, a messenger came to recount what had happened to Hippolytus as a result of his father's curse. We do not know whether or not Hippolytus appeared on stage again, as he does in the second play. As for Phaedra, she probably killed herself when she realised that the truth would be revealed. Seneca's Phaedra kills herself out of remorse, after a voluntary confession, but we do not know who revealed the truth to Theseus – Phaedra, her nurse or some deity, as in the second play. Like the second, the first play prophesied the establishment of a cult of Hippolytus (fragment 446).

It is often assumed that Sophocles' *Phaedra* came between the two Euripidean plays, although this is pure conjecture. Still, the basic sequence of events, from the approach to Hippolytus, through the false accusation, Theseus' curse and Hippolytus' destruction was presumably common to all three. It is also usually assumed that, as with Euripides' other *Hippolytus*,[10] the scene of Sophocles' play was Athens, since there are some logical difficulties associated with the Trozenian setting in the extant play, but Sophocles' work was generally less controversial than Euripides', and this play seems not to have left any mark on the sensibilities of Aristophanes or others. Scholars therefore suggest that the initial approach to him, as in the second play, was not made by Phaedra but by some go-between. A number of fragments are somewhat reminiscent of lines in the extant play, but since they lack any context or speaker, it is hard to gauge the significance of superficial similarities. Still, fragment 679 refers to what is 'shameful' and 680 to 'troubles sent by the gods', a tone which resembles that of the Euripidean play, while 684 speaks of the power of love that conquers even Zeus, and recalls the advice of the Nurse at *Hippolytus* 451ff. that Phaedra should gratify her love.

Theseus was certainly away in Hades when Phaedra fell in love, since 686 is a dialogue between Theseus and someone else: 'So you are alive, and did not go to die under the earth?' 'Yes; fortune does not compel [death] before it is fated.' It is often conjectured that Sophocles laid little, if any, emphasis on the impious aspects of the adventure, and it is sometimes suggested that, if this Theseus had been absent for so long that he had been given up for dead, the charge of adultery against Phaedra might have been partly mitigated. Perhaps Phaedra's motivation for the false accusation was the preservation of her honour, as in the extant play, and panic or shame at her husband's unexpected return led her to accuse Hippolytus.

We know even less about Sophocles' treatment of the theme than Euripides', although there may have been more in common between Sophocles' Phaedra and Euripides' second Phaedra than between Euripides' two Phaedras. When he came to write his second version of the play, Euripides would have had his

34

first Phaedra in mind and (depending on the chronology) perhaps also that of Sophocles. The 'what' of the myth was, to a large extent, determined for him; but the 'how' was his to alter, to contradict himself, to tell a story that was quite different from, and yet the same as, the story that he first told. He would have appreciated such a paradox, inherent in Greek mythical narratives in a culture in which the spoken, not the written word was still dominant. There was no correct version of the Hippolytus myth, except in so far as it concerned Phaedra's love and Hippolytus' death. The rest was up to the individual to create.

3

A Summary of the Play

The *Hippolytus* is set in Trozen, outside Theseus' palace. Statues of Aphrodite and Artemis, the two goddesses who frame the action of the play, stand on either side of the *skênê* building, and Aphrodite gives the prologue speech. She emphasises her power among mortals, and warns that she respects those who honour her, but has no mercy on those who do not, because it is divine nature to crave honour from mortals. Her treatment of Hippolytus will exemplify this principle, for he alone in Trozen calls her vile, and repudiates love and marriage. Instead, she says, he prefers to go hunting with her sister Artemis, with whom he has a relationship 'more than mortal'. Although she denies that she is jealous of their association, she seeks revenge for his disrespect to her. She has been laying her plans for some time, and everything will come to fruition on this day.

Hippolytus had been living with his great-grandfather Pittheus (24ff.), but when he visited Athens to participate in the mysteries at Eleusis,[1] Phaedra fell in love with him and even erected a temple of Aphrodite in his honour. When Theseus had to leave Athens for a year to expiate killing the Pallantidae,[2] he and his wife settled in Trozen, his other kingdom through his maternal grandfather Pittheus. Now her love has made Phaedra ill, but she has told nobody why she is sick. Aphrodite goes on to summarise – not entirely accurately – what will happen (41ff.): she will reveal all to Theseus, and he will curse his son by using one of the three wishes that his divine father Poseidon once gave him. Though Phaedra is honourable, she will die anyway, since Aphrodite is set on revenge. Hippolytus enters just as she withdraws with the prophecy that this is his last day alive.

The unsuspecting Hippolytus and his band of fellow-hunters sing a hymn to Artemis (58ff.), to whom he dedicates a garland from an 'untouched' meadow watered by the goddess Aidôs.[3] The meadow is for those who need no teaching, but who are naturally virtuous in all matters: 'the bad' are excluded from this paradise. Hippolytus places the garland on the statue's head, claiming that he alone of all mortals is privileged to be with Artemis, even though he can only hear her voice and does not see her form. He ends with a wish that he may end his life as he began it.

His subsequent exchange with an old attendant reveals both another side of his concern for purity and the truth of Aphrodite's complaints of his hostility to her (88ff.) In a passage of *stichomythia* in which he seems nervous about his master's reaction, the attendant first gets him to admit that arrogance is an unattractive quality among men and gods and then asks him why he does not worship a proud goddess.[4] Hippolytus seems, or pretends to seem, not to know that he means Aphrodite, but when he can avoid the topic no longer, he asserts boldly, 'I worship her from afar, since I am pure.' Although the old man persists, and warns him that all gods need worship, Hippolytus expresses distaste for a god 'worshipped at night' (106), and dismisses his concerns. Instead, he turns to his attendants, ordering them in to dinner and to tend the horses. With a final, 'And to that Kypris of yours, I bid plenty of farewells', he leaves the scene. The attendant prays to Aphrodite, asking her to forgive Hippolytus' inexperience, since 'gods should be wiser than mortals'.

At line 121, the *parodos* begins, as a chorus of Trozenian women sing that they were at the stream washing clothes, when they heard from a friend of queen Phaedra's illness. For three days she has not eaten and wishes to die. They speculate about possible causes of her pain. Perhaps she is possessed by Pan, or perhaps she has neglected the goddess Dictynna.[5] Perhaps Theseus has been unfaithful or she has received bad news from her family in Crete. Finally they suggest that gynaecological trouble might be to blame and that she should ask Artemis' help.

Phaedra's old Nurse now brings her outside at her demand for fresh air (176). She cannot cope with her restless patient, and complains about her hard lot. At line 198, Phaedra finally opens her mouth and longs to run free in the countryside, and to hunt or tame horses. The Nurse is horrified at what she interprets as a delirious wish, unfit for an Athenian queen.

At 239, Phaedra recollects herself in embarrassment at her previous words. Since she can bear neither madness nor reality she wants to die. For the Nurse, life is not worth living without Phaedra and she opines that since partings are painful and inevitable, mortals should not get too attached to one another, but be moderate in all things, including affection. Phaedra sinks back, exhausted, and the Chorus prevail upon the Nurse to try once more to discover what is wrong. Against Phaedra's stead-fast silence, she tries various approaches, and eventually reminds her of her responsibility to her children (304f.). Her death will endanger their claim to the throne, since Theseus' illegitimate son Hippolytus might seize power. At his name, Phaedra, silent for 60 lines, cannot control herself, and cries 'alas'.

It quickly becomes clear that the succession is not at issue, as we move into the long stretch of *stichomythia* (315ff.) that culminates in Phaedra's confession. At first, she speaks rid-dlingly of an inner pollution. Her enigmatic words encourage the Nurse to persist and their conversation gains momentum. The Nurse plays her trump card at 326 by supplicating[6] her to tell her the truth. Phaedra demurs at first, but her obscure allusions to shame only excite the Nurse's curiosity. Eventually at 335, Phaedra accepts her supplication, and seals her own fate. Even now, she cannot approach the subject directly, and begins with musings on her mother Pasiphae's love for a bull and her 'poor sister' Ariadne's romantic misfortunes. She names herself as the third in her family to be unlucky in love. She wants the Nurse to divine the truth from these cryptic words so that she need not be explicit, but naturally, the Nurse is baffled and Phaedra abandons this line of talk. At 347 she starts again, with a general question – 'What do men say love is?' and the Nurse catches on – her mistress is in love – with whom? Phaedra's response encapsulates her ambivalence between revelation and secrecy: 'Whoever he is – the son of the Amazon –' and the Nurse finally says the fateful name – 'You mean Hippolytus?' The Nurse is so horrified that for her, as for Phaedra, suicide seems the only solution. The Chorus, similarly appalled, sing a short lyric (362ff.).

At 373, however, Phaedra commands the stage with a long speech that contrasts with her lyric utterances:[7] her weakness is forgotten. This Phaedra is a thinker who has often wondered why human lives go wrong. It is, she concludes, not because we do not know what good is, but because we do not carry it out, whether through laziness or through preferring pleasures, such as conversation, leisure, and – rather surprisingly – shame (*aidôs*) to the good. They (whether pleasures or shame is unclear) are of two types: one not bad, the other the destroyer of houses. If we knew the difference, there would be a different word for each. After this complex utterance, she explains her actions in the light of her conclusions (388ff.) When she first fell in love, she decided that it would be most noble to keep silent, and then to conquer her feelings through self-control. Then, since this was hopeless, she decided to kill herself. Her explanation of her suicide plan is significant: she wants neither to do what is glorious in secret, nor to be observed while acting shamefully (403-4). She then launches into a self-righteous tirade against adulterous women and their hypocrisy, trying to distance herself from behaving as they do, before collecting herself and returning to her explanation of her intention to die. Never will she be caught shaming her husband or children. The Chorus are impressed at her self-control, and praise her noble words.

But now (433) the Nurse has had time to think again, and since she loves Phaedra and wants an easy life, recommends that she gratify her love. Many people fall in love, after all, and Aphrodite cannot be ignored. Moreover, even the gods fall in love, and if they do it, how can it be wrong? Human life is imperfect, dubious love affairs are the norm, and if you have more good than bad as a mortal, you are doing well. She characterises Phaedra's attempts to resist her love as mere presumption towards the gods, since a god has willed it upon her, and suggests that she should cast a spell to make Hippolytus return her love.

The Chorus scent trouble and say that the Nurse is more practical, but Phaedra is more honourable (482-5). Phaedra agrees with them: one should not say what is pleasing – a significant admission – but what brings honour. But the Nurse cares only that she should live: if Phaedra could have restrained herself, she would not have recommended this course, but since she cannot, and needs 'the man' (491), she must not be allowed to die. Phaedra begs her to speak no more 'fine words about shameful things', since she cannot resist much longer. The Nurse knows she has won, and mentions that she has some love-charms at home that will end the illness 'without shame or harm' to her. Phaedra believes her, although not without misgivings, and begs her not to tell Hippolytus. The Nurse assures her that she will arrange everything well and Phaedra protests no more.

In the first *stasimon* (525-64), the Chorus reflect on Love as a force of beauty and of destruction. Phaedra remains on stage listening at the palace door, and when the Chorus have finished, she realises that the Nurse has revealed her secret to Hippolytus. In a brief exchange as the Chorus ask what is happening, Phaedra states that the Nurse has destroyed her and she must kill herself at once (565-600). Her resigned iambic trimeters contrast with their excited lyric utterances. She is still on stage as Hippolytus bursts out and confronts the Nurse (601ff.). He has never directly spoken to Phaedra.

He threatens to expose Phaedra, and the Nurse's supplications have no apparent effect on him. When she reminds him that he had sworn an oath of silence before she revealed Phaedra's secret, he replies, 'My tongue swore, my mind remains unsworn.' In answer to her appeal for understanding, he begins a violent denunciation of women (616ff.): although he is aware of Phaedra (cf. 907), he cannot directly address such a polluting presence. He wishes for a world in which men could simply buy children and avoid all contact with women, and offers as a 'proof' that women are evil the fact that their fathers 'sell' them to husbands with dowries (627f.). Worst of all are clever women, for they are more wicked, and it would be better if they were silent and kept locked up under the guardianship of wild beasts. Eventually (651) he addresses the Nurse directly: he feels polluted by even hearing such talk. Only his piety saves her, since – in spite of his first reaction – he will keep his oath. He will leave the country until Theseus' return, and then watch how the Nurse and Phaedra behave. Finally he claims that he will never stop hating women, 'Not even if people say I am always talking about them', since someone should either teach them virtue or let him trample on them some more (664-8).

After a brief lament for the wretchedness of women and her own fate (669f.), Phaedra upbraids the Nurse for her meddling, and laments that she will die dishonourably. Even now, the optimistic Nurse points out that her plan might have worked in other circumstances, and has had a new idea, but Phaedra has heard enough. Instead, she swears the Chorus to secrecy regarding a plan she has for passing on an honourable life to her sons. Echoing the Nurse's false assurance to her at 521 that she will arrange things well, Phaedra announces her intention to do the same (709), so as not to disgrace her family or Theseus. To her intention to die, she adds ominously that her death will cause trouble for another, so that sharing in her pain, 'he will learn virtue' (728-31).

The second *stasimon* (732-75) is full of foreboding, as the Chorus long to be far away, lament Phaedra's ill-omened marriage and prophesy her death. A voice is then heard from inside (776), announcing that she has hanged herself. Theseus now returns from an expedition to an oracle (790). He has been expecting a happy welcome and is shocked to hear sounds of mourning. His first concern is for Pittheus, and then for his children. Phaedra is only his third thought, but once the Chorus tell him that she has hanged herself and the body is revealed on the *ekkyklêma*, he is horrified and, in a gesture reversing Hippolytus' placing the garland on Artemis' statue, he flings the garland on his head onto the ground (806f.). He then pours forth a torrent of lamentation for a beloved wife, in which metre underlines mood, as Euripides mingles dochmiacs (a metre associated with intense emotion) with iambic trimeters, a combination appropriate for a strong man trying to control grief. Throughout his 50 lines of lamentation, the audience is anxious to know what will happen next. At 856, he notices a writing tablet attached to Phaedra's wrist. He does not immediately read it and speculates instead that it contains a request that he not remarry, but at last, he reads her posthumous accusation of rape against his son, and immediately invokes Poseidon to destroy him, adding exile from his kingdom as an additional punishment. Since the Chorus are bound by their oath to Phaedra they can only advise him not to be too hasty (891-2).

3. A Summary of the Play

At 902 Hippolytus arrives, and a bruising encounter between father and son takes place in which each communicates at, rather than with, the other. Just as Hippolytus could not bring himself to address the Nurse immediately, but denounced all women, so Theseus launches a general attack on hypocrites, wondering why reason cannot be imposed on the stupid (916ff.). Hippolytus is baffled by his outburst, so he tries again. This time, he suggests that men should have two voices, so that dishonest speech would always be refuted by the truth (925f.). Hippolytus realises that these apparently general remarks might be directed at him, and asks who has been slandering him. Theseus interprets this as pure hypocrisy, and in more speculatory fantasy, imagines that the gods will have to create a whole other world for wicked and dishonest men. Finally, at 943, he directs his remarks straight at Hippolytus, saying that he has been 'convicted' of being thoroughly evil. He mockingly flings Hippolytus' own protestations of virtue back at him, accusing him of hypocrisy and false asceticism (948ff.).

The next part of his denunciation has a decidedly legal flavour (958ff.). Under sophistic influence, Athenian forensic orators use arguments based on probability as much as on material evidence. Thus Theseus imagines a possible defence for Hippolytus against Phaedra's charge, and then contemptuously refutes each imagined possibility. Does he think that Phaedra's death will save him? Not at all – it makes his wickedness seem all the likelier. Did she kill herself to spite him, out of hatred for his bastard status? Ridiculous! Does he think that women are more sexually wanton than men? No – Theseus knows that young men are just as prone to Aphrodite's influence. In any case, all this is irrelevant, since Phaedra's corpse is unambiguous evidence of his guilt. Once more, therefore, Theseus condemns his son to exile, since his heroic reputation will be compromised if he does not take vigorous action.

The tone of Hippolytus' speech for the defence (983ff.) does not help him. As though addressing a public meeting, he asserts that he is unskilled at speaking before 'the masses', but rather before a few wiser contemporaries, since those who shine among the masses typically do badly among the wise. He then asserts that no man is purer than he. If Theseus is not convinced by this assertion then he should consider what is likely. Just as Theseus set up and shot down a sequence of hypothetical arguments for the defence, his son offers something similar (1009ff.). Was Phaedra the most beautiful of women? Did he wish to acquire a larger inheritance? Did he wish to be king? For Hippolytus, the answer is clearly no. But these assertions without further proof do not convince the Athenian king, especially when Hippolytus adds that kingship is not attractive to anyone sensible. His ambitions are very different from those pursued by Theseus: he wants to be first in the Greek games, and to associate with like-minded young men, avoiding political prominence. He wishes for a witness as virtuous as he is to prove his innocence, and swears a great oath that he is blameless. All the while, he keeps the promised oath of silence, although he does hint at something that it is 'not right' for him to mention (1033), and ends with the intriguing claim that Phaedra was virtuous while unable to exercise virtue, while he, though virtuous, cannot exercise his virtue well.

This riddle is surely intended to pique Theseus' interest. Unfortunately, he is so sure of Hippolytus' egregious hypocrisy that he ignores it, and again threatens him with exile. Only now does Hippolytus realise that he is in trouble, and Theseus once more cites the allegedly irrefutable evidence of Phaedra's letter. To his son's plea that he at least seek proof from a diviner, he retorts that he 'bids many farewells' to these, dismissing them just as Hippolytus dismissed Aphrodite (1059, cf. 113). Hippolytus appeals once more to the gods, and wishes that he could tell the truth, but again, Theseus does not take his cue. The encounter is in effect at an end here, although it runs for about another 20 lines, as Hippolytus makes two final impossible wishes. To his wish that the walls of the house could vouch for him, Theseus sneers that he can only rely on voiceless witnesses. When he longs to stand beside himself to weep at his own innocence (1079), Theseus replies that his words are typical of someone who honours himself more than his parents. At last, Hippolytus resigns himself to leaving Athens and Trozen, once more asserting that they will never see a more virtuous man.

In the third *stasimon* (1104-50), the Chorus express unease at the uncertainty of human life, and hope for fortunate lives and honest and flexible minds. They draw these conclusions from Hippolytus' troubles, and lament his imminent exile. Then a messenger arrives, and says that Hippolytus 'is no more'. Theseus, still angry, assumes that another wronged husband has hurt him, but the messenger explains that his own horses destroyed him, due to Theseus' curse. Theseus appears shocked (1169ff.): 'Oh gods and Poseidon, so you really were my father.' In a detailed speech, which dwells on Hippolytus' anguish, the messenger explains that a huge bull from the sea reared up in front of his chariot, and pursued him relentlessly, so that in spite of his horsemanship, he eventually crashed on a rock and was dragged along against the rocks. He inspires particular pity by directly quoting the young man's distressed pleas to his beloved horses (1240f.). Theseus' reaction is quiet and neutral: though he was pleased at Hippolytus' punishment, out of respect for the gods and his son, he is neither glad nor sorry for what has happened. He wishes to see him one more time, so as to force him to confess to Phaedra's rape.

The Chorus sing a brief hymn in praise of Aphrodite and her power (1269f.). Not Aphrodite but Artemis then appears, and the last part of the play begins. She coldly rebukes Theseus for his hasty conduct. She has come so that Hippolytus may die absolved, and to reveal what she calls Phaedra's 'wild lust, or sort of nobility' (1300). In a parallel to Aphrodite's earlier account of what will happen, she explains what actually happened. Theseus is horrified, especially at her insistence that his own curse is killing his son. He longs for death, but now she relents, and puts the real blame upon Aphrodite, explaining that she could have done nothing to prevent the tragedy since gods cannot thwart one another's purposes. Theseus is ultimately forgiven on the grounds of ignorance, and Artemis even expresses sorrow for his grief: she too feels sorrow, since 'gods do not rejoice when the pious die', although they punish the bad (1325-41).

Hippolytus' servants bring in their dying master in a scene which mirrors Phaedra's first entrance. He remains unrepentant to Aphrodite, and blames the horses, Zeus or his father but never his own intransigence for his sufferings. To himself (1364), he is still 'the pious and god-fearing one'. At 1398, Artemis talks to him – even now, he cannot actually see her. She agrees that his plight is wretched, and expresses sorrow for his fate, but she cannot change it, nor, as a divinity, may she even weep for him. They agree that Aphrodite is solely to blame. When he oversteps the mark by wishing that mortals could curse the gods (1416), Artemis intervenes and offers him the consolation prizes of a revenge attack on Aphrodite's favourite Adonis, and his own cult at Trozen (1420ff.) Such cold comforts seem curiously appropriate for a life which is beautiful but devoid of human warmth.

At 1433-4 Artemis finally absolves the human characters: 'It is natural that humans make mistakes when the gods grant it thus.' She must not see Hippolytus die, but before she leaves, she insists on a reconciliation between father and son. Hippolytus comments that she leaves their 'long association' with ease (1441). Such is the gulf between men and gods. The play ends with a dialogue between the two broken humans as they attempt to comfort each other. Theseus acknowledges his son's

piety while Hippolytus grants forgiveness to his father before
he dies, and the Chorus briefly lament the loss to the city that
his death has brought (1462-6).

4

The Major Themes of the Play

Introduction: duality, plot and characterisation

The central theme of the *Hippolytus* is quintessential to tragedy: a human being with an exaggerated idea of his own merits
transgresses against a divinity who re-establishes the divine-
human hierarchy by crushing him. Onto this classic structure
is grafted another traditional plot – which occurs in Irish,
Icelandic and Italian stories as well as several Euripidean
tragedies, including the first *Hippolytus* – of the attempted
seduction of a virtuous youth by a wicked woman. The mixture
of two plotlines creates an extremely unusual play, which main-
tains an emphasis on duality and ambiguity throughout.

Duality is innate in the structure of even simple Greek
sentences, which are often of the form, 'on the one hand ... on
the other', but it is especially prominent in sophistic thought. As
we saw in Chapter 1, the sophist Protagoras asserted that
everything has a stronger and a weaker argument, and that one
can always be turned into the other. The essential element of the
story of Phaedra and her stepson is that she fell in love with him
and caused his destruction. This story makes her 'bad', and
Hippolytus 'good'. This is the standard version of the story
(remaining so long after 428) and may be called the 'stronger'
argument in that the moral characters of the two seem obvious.
Yet on reading the play, the apparently obvious becomes less so:
Aphrodite herself calls Phaedra 'honourable' (47), but makes

48

4. The Major Themes of the Play

her fall in love with Hippolytus anyway to have her revenge on him. He does not deserve his fate, yet many people have found his elitism and belief in his own virtue unattractive. Euripides reinvents the story, so that what is apparently clear – Phaedra is evil, and Hippolytus virtuous – is less so: the weaker argument is now the stronger. Later critics assumed that Euripides wrote the second *Hippolytus* to counter hostile reactions to his earlier version: this cannot be disproved, but at least as plausible is the idea that he was attracted by the intellectual challenge of dramatising the same story with a completely different moral focus. In fact, this is not the only time that he would twist myth like this. In *Medea*, an infanticidal mother is disturbingly sympathetic when pitted against a dishonest Greek hero; in *Helen*, Greece's most famous adulteress exemplifies conjugal fidelity.

An Athenian audience about to view a play called *Hippolytus* had expectations about it, especially if they had seen the earlier play. In the extant play, Euripides makes strenuous efforts – sometimes at the cost of creating minor awkwardness in the plot – to baffle such expectations. Throughout the play, he makes the audience think that they know *what* must happen next, while surprising them as to *how* it happens. Forty lines into the play, Aphrodite tells them what they will see, yet it is not a full account nor is it exactly what happens. She does not reveal the truth to Theseus, as she promises at 42, while her order of events – revelation to Theseus, death of Hippolytus, death of Phaedra – is designed to mislead the audience into assuming that its chronology will replicate that of the first play. Her imperfect revelations both remove suspense and increase it. From their knowledge of the myth, the audience know that Hippolytus must die, and Aphrodite assures them that this expectation will be met. Their expectations will also be telling them, however, that Phaedra will falsely accuse him of rape, yet an 'honourable' Phaedra who is suffering in silence throws such

49

expectations into doubt. Throughout the play Euripides makes us wait for what we know must happen – there is a lengthy delay between Phaedra's arrival on stage and her speech, Theseus does not read her letter immediately, and so on. The play sometimes seems like a comment on the nature of myth itself, where no version is 'right' or 'wrong' so that the protean and the predictable are both innate.

The sophists demonstrated that what seems to be natural or obvious need not always be so, and were fascinated by linguistic ambiguity and the fallibility of human perception. Thus, whereas in the first *Hippolytus*, the terms of the plot surely dictated the moral characters of its agents to make a wanton and destructive Phaedra, an ill-used and virtuous Hippolytus, and a hasty and violent Theseus, the second *Hippolytus* colours moral praise and blame more subtly. The favourable portrayal of Phaedra is a most unusual presentation of a notorious woman, and even though eventually she behaves just as badly as ever, she does so only after strenuous efforts to avoid doing so and after betrayal by the Nurse. Hippolytus lives a beautiful and pure life, but he is fanatical, and although his punishment is undeserved, there is a causal connection between his attitude to Aphrodite and his suffering. The Nurse has no stable moral code and sets the tragedy in motion, and yet her love for her mistress is genuine. Though Theseus must pronounce the curse that causes his son's death, he does so without fully realising that it will be efficacious. Thus all of the four characters whose actions together precipitate the tragedy can be viewed in a dual aspect, both favourably and unfavourably.

No individual is either fully guilty or fully innocent, and they act from motives that are good but rest on false belief, from ignorance that is not wholly culpable, or from ambiguous motives that are carefully poised between admirable and wicked. The Nurse's understanding of Hippolytus is so limited that she thinks that she can persuade him into an affair with Phaedra.

Theseus takes his wife's letter as clear evidence of his son's guilt. Should he have known better? That is not clear. Does Phaedra accuse Hippolytus for her children's sake or because she has been rejected? Again, it is not clear. At 717f. her motives look honourable, but her final threat that by sharing in her trouble 'someone' will learn wisdom seems vengeful. Hardest of all to judge is the extraordinary character of Hippolytus, like no other in Greek literature. He has a lack of sympathy with others and a great sense of his own virtue, and yet he is young and inexperienced, and his life has great beauty in many ways. Is it not understandable that someone of his type would be outraged by Phaedra's adulterous quasi-incestuous passion? Just because he is devoted to Artemis at Aphrodite's expense, how could she be so petty as to take pains to punish him so hideously? Moreover, although both Aphrodite and Theseus are hostile to him, neither is the most reliable witness, and by contrast, the Chorus, his companions and the messenger greatly admire him. Must we really side with Aphrodite and Theseus against them?

The ambiguity hanging over all the participants is exemplified by Artemis' final absolution: 'It is natural that humans make mistakes when the gods grant it thus' (1433-4). While it is common for divinities to appear at the end of a tragedy to explain why that tragedy happened, they do not usually acquit everyone of any real guilt in what has happened and blame another god: they are usually less generous and behave more as Artemis initially does to Theseus (1283ff., 1313ff.). Ultimately, the tragedy is Aphrodite's fault, yet even she is justified, at least by divine law, because of the disrespect shown to her (6f., cf. 1340f.).

It is sometimes claimed that the gods of the *Hippolytus* are essentially personifications of forces in the human psyche, so that one could have a perfectly comprehensible play without the divine epiphanies. This is not really true, because the motivation for Phaedra's sudden love and the effects of Theseus' curse

are incomprehensible in a world without divinities who intervene in human lives, but certainly all the characters do behave
very plausibly once Aphrodite has set up her plot. The Nurse
wants to keep her beloved charge alive at all costs, Phaedra
accuses Hippolytus because she fears unjust damage to her
reputation, Theseus jumps to understandable conclusions. It is
as though Aphrodite knows her characters and their weak-
nesses – notably the obsession of both Phaedra and Hippolytus
with reputation – and works through these to destroy them. But
since Aphrodite has caused Phaedra's love, and because she has
hitherto been an honourable woman, who, at least until the
Nurse persuades her to reveal her secret, would put death
before dishonour, she is somewhat absolved of responsibility for
her love, though not of the false accusation.

If, as I assume, the first *Hippolytus* laid particular emphasis
on the scandalous aspects of Phaedra's passion, then it would
have portrayed a female sexuality that would have fed many
Athenians' worst anxieties. Such a portrayal is consistent with
the Euripidean realism in which the portrayal of grand heroes
of mythical tradition as more ordinary men causes unease in
the audience by making them a little too close to real life and
real concerns. Indeed, Aristophanes counters Euripides' defence
that his first Phaedra was realistically portrayed with the
indignant statement that realism of this kind is inappropriate
for the stage (*Frogs* 1052-3). By contrast, the second *Hippolytus*
would be presenting not only less scandalous material, but also
material slightly distanced from ordinary life by the prominent
role given to divinity. Moreover, a Trozenian rather than Athenian setting has particular advantages. Tragedy is very rarely
set in Athens, and when it is, Athenians are usually those who
help victims, rather than the victims themselves. A Trozenian
setting enables that combination of sympathy and distance
which is vital for a successful tragedy. The setting actually
causes small oddities in the plot which are best explicable on

the assumption that Euripides has transferred certain details of a story earlier set in Athens. For example, Aphrodite explains the presence of Phaedra's temple of Hippolytus in Athens by saying that when Hippolytus visited Athens from Trozen, Phaedra fell in love, built the temple and then left for Trozen (24-33). An Athenian setting avoids this convoluted explanation. Similarly, the exile of Theseus for the murder of the Pallantidae explains his presence with Hippolytus in Trozen but contradicts standard tradition, in which Theseus is born in Trozen but goes to Athens when he grows up, kills the Pallantidae during his father Aegeus' lifetime, and never returns to Trozen.

Whereas we are accustomed to detailed miniatures of personality in much modern film and theatre, the conditions of Greek tragic performance necessitate a much broader approach to characterisation in which realism is not always the playwright's most important concern. Even so, Euripides is somewhat closer to modern drama than his predecessors in his obvious interest in individual psychological motivation for its own sake. The *Hippolytus* balances the fantastic of the divine framework with realism in the way that the characters are made to behave, and I suspect that this realism is a necessary result of his having so extensively altered the original moral focus of the story. The first play's plot would have been so archetypal that it would have driven and determined its characterisation: in the second play, the plot depends more on individual motivation, so that Phaedra and others are convincingly portrayed as the sort of people whose characters impel them to act so as to mean well – for the most part – while actually causing disaster.

Phaedra

The first play is a kind of darker background against which the new, improved Phaedra of the extant play shines. This Phaedra struggles nobly against divinely-inspired emotions, and is prepared even to die to avoid dishonour to herself and her family. When the Chorus and Nurse are trying to find out what is wrong, their guess that Theseus has been unfaithful to her (151, cf. 321) may actually be a sly reference to the first play in which she used his adulteries to justify her conduct.[1] Similarly, while her predecessor actually propositioned Hippolytus on stage, this Phaedra is so appalled by her feelings that only a determined onslaught from the Nurse finally reveals her secret. Even then, she cannot say Hippolytus' name aloud, and manoeuvres the Nurse into saying it instead. She is obsessed with honour, the very quality that her predecessor signally lacked. When she first appears, she is weak through fasting, punishing her body for its dreadful demands (123ff., 176ff.). In one of the play's many paradoxes concerning the nature of true purity, she is keeping her body 'pure' of food (138) while actually approaching the ritually impure state of death. Hippolytus too regards his abstention from bodily desires as true purity (102, 1003), and he too is mistaken in his belief. Deliriously, she yearns to be outside, taming horses[2] and hunting, but once her delirium subsides, she expresses shame (244) at her words: she has the moral consciousness to be embarrassed by her blatant expression of desire, even though her words are quite obscure to the Nurse and Chorus, and she tries to behave as her regal status demands. Her words at 247f. foreshadow the conclusions to which she says she has come in calmer mood at 373ff.: sanity is painful, but since madness is an evil, she should die.

Although she is apparently trying to keep her secret, fewer than 200 lines later we are on the brink of the tragedy. Her change of heart is caused by accepting the Nurse's supplication (324f.). Since we know that this will prove disastrous, we tend to feel that she too should have known, and the sincerity of her desire for honour is thrown into doubt. Is her acceptance of the supplication just a handy excuse for revealing what she longs to reveal and knows she should not? Acceptance of a suppliant is an important moral obligation in Greece, but the obligation is often a matter of life and death – for example, when a suppliant is fleeing an oppressor – so it could be argued that, since the Nurse's supplication is not of this kind, Phaedra should have regarded silence as the higher good and rejected her. Well before the supplication, in fact, her speech excites the Nurse's curiosity far more than it truly stops further questioning. Who could not wish to know more when told that 'My hands are pure, but my mind is polluted' (317)? At 329 and 331, her words are thrilling in their obscurity – she is doing wrong, but 'The matter is bringing honour to me' and 'Out of shameful things, I am making good.' Presumably the only good that could be made out of her shameful passion is some means of evading the revelation of the truth, yet Phaedra can neither be silent nor speak directly.[3] Although subtle psychologising is generally considered alien to Greek drama, I think that the whole scene makes sense in terms of a conflict between her outward desire for honour and the desire that she is failing to repress, and that even if a Greek tragedian could not possibly have conceptualised a conflict between conscious and subconscious, Euripides' portrayal of her ambiguous revelations at least *resembles* a modern writer's portrayal of someone whose subconscious lurks beneath her stated desires and subverts them. There is, however, also a sophistic aspect to the scene: accepting a supplication is usually good and brings good results – in this play, it is what causes the disaster. Therefore, the stronger argument (accepting a suppliant is good) is turned into the weaker one (supplication can lead to disaster).

Much of Phaedra's great speech of 373ff. concerns moral conduct, and 373-87 concentrate specifically on the nature of *aidôs*, a word that has no English equivalent, but shame, modesty, reverence and respect are all part of it (cf. Chapter 3, pp. 37 and 133n3) and it is the sort of feeling that the first Phaedra lacked. This speech has garnered more critical attention than any other in the play, and this chapter will offer my own interpretation of it, leaving other possibilities for Chapter 5, because, though its outlines are clear – many people know what is right but do not do it, but I, Phaedra, will do the right thing – its specifics, textually, in interpretation and its relationship to the rest of the play, are complex. At 65 lines, it is by far her longest speech, so it ought to offer the most clues as to her motivations. Interpreters often consider it in the light of the whole play, and try to show that 373-87 explain why she has confessed her love to the Nurse, since the confession will cause the tragedy. Later in the speech (403-4, 420-1), Euripides has certainly provided hints of the motivations which will lead her to make her false accusation. But it seems to me that Phaedra should not know beforehand that the Nurse is going to betray her, so that even if 373-87 are retrospectively relevant to the whole play, they must also be comprehensible purely in the context of 1-372 and of the rest of this speech. Part of its function is to reassure her household that she will not disgrace herself or them. As we have seen, she has already considered suicide the least disgraceful way of avoiding the consequences of her love.

This Phaedra is not a sex-mad hussy, but a thinker, familiar with contemporary ethical speculation, whose speech is full of intellectual terminology. She has spent nights thinking about why human lives go wrong, and has concluded that it is not because we do not know how to behave, but because we do not act in accordance with our knowledge. This seems to recall, but contradict, Socrates' famous view that virtue depends on knowledge, so that true knowledge will bring about correct action (Plato *Protagoras* 352d). Euripides is less optimistic: for him, knowing what to do will not always mean that we actually do it. Indeed, his Medea makes a claim similar to Phaedra's immediately before she kills her children (*Medea* 1078f.). In one of the ironies of this play, in spite of this speech, Phaedra becomes the supreme example of someone who does know what is right but manifestly fails to do it.

'We know what is good and understand it but we do not carry it out fully, some out of laziness and others preferring some other pleasure to what is noble.' For Phaedra, nobility is a pleasure,[4] as is appropriate for a woman who has previously lived a life in which right conduct, its appearance and an excellent reputation have all been synonymous. She cites leisure and gossip as pleasures which lead us astray from honour – pleasures presumably familiar to an aristocratic woman such as she – but then adds 'shame' (*aidôs*) to the list. Since *aidôs* is most commonly defined as something that prevents wrongdoing, by inhibiting self-assertion, her claim that it can inhibit right action is surprising.[5]

She continues (386-7), 'One of these is not bad, but the other is the ruin of houses. If we could be sure of what was opportune, the two would not be spelled with the same letters.'[6] It is disputed whether 'these' refers to two kinds of shame or two of pleasure – the syntax is ambiguous, and the arguments for neither are entirely conclusive. However, the assertion that some pleasures are good and some bad seems banal in comparison with the idea that shame is ambiguous between good and bad. Moreover, just as accepting a suppliant is normally good but brings disaster for Phaedra, if shame normally helps right conduct by inhibiting bad, but fails to do so in this play, once more the stronger and weaker arguments are being reversed.

But if shame is a pleasure with two manifestations, one not bad, the other the ruin of houses, what are they? Many suggestions have been made – a selection is given in the next chapter – but none command absolute agreement. Sometimes, the destructive *aidôs* is assumed to be that of 335 when she says *aidoumai* (I respect it) in accepting the supplication which will destroy her. While later in the play she is indeed uneasy about what she has done (518f.), such a fear is surely out of place this early. Instead, we need an interpretation that is directly relevant to her situation at this moment, and so I suggest that the *aidôs* which destroys houses is the *aidôs* that is impelling her to kill herself, since the rest of this speech is essentially an explanation of why she must die. In this instance, the 'shame' that is motivating her is 'not bad' because it will preserve her good name – a pleasure – but it is 'the ruin of houses', since, from the entry of the Chorus down to this point, it is made plain that Phaedra is the centre of their universe and that the disaster which threatens her threatens the entire house (250-1, 329, 355, 365, cf. 817-18, 823-5, 846-7).

This is, however, not the standard interpretation of the speech, and it demands that we assume a lapse of logic in her argument, whereby she changes tack slightly from 'things which prevent us from right action' to 'things in her life which are potentially harmful', among which is *aidôs*. Clearly, though, her meditations on virtue have precipitated her decision to die, since she continues (388), '*Therefore* since I happen to think this, no magic charm could have made me change my mind.' She explains that when she first fell in love, she considered how she could endure it. She tried silence unsuccessfully, then self-control (*sôphronein*) but since neither has worked, she has decided to die. She is explicit at 402ff.: 'I do not want either to be invisible when acting honourably nor visible when acting shamefully' (403-4). These words are the first sign that her idea of honour may lead her to trouble: while for a Greek audience, much more than for one in a world influenced by Christianity, virtue does have a strong external dimension, so that moral status partly depends on reputation among others, appearance and reality are not always identical, and the disjunction between them is a major theme of this play.[7] Care for her reputation as synonymous with her true moral character has worked for Phaedra up until now, but the harmony between perception and reality is fatally damaged where Aphrodite has meddled.

Once she has made her decision, she grows increasingly impassioned, so that her death is no longer a 'burden on the house' but a glorious act that will ensure her reputation forever. Euripides conveys the immense effort that her struggles are taking, both by emphasising her physical sickness and – with acute psychological insight – by her tirades (407ff.) against women who lack self-control. Hippolytus' later condemnation of all women will even echo her denunciations of adulterous women here – her 'I hate the virtuous ones' (*misô de kai tas sôphronas* [413f.]) resembles 640 and his 'I hate the clever one' (*sophên de misô*). She dwells obsessively on deeds that 'should make their houses cry aloud in horror' (418), and expresses her intention, by contrast, of saving her family from dishonour (419-27): her passage from uncertainty to violent certainty is most effective. But we know, in spite of her best efforts, that she cannot thwart a vengeful goddess.

Although she claims that her good name in relation to Theseus and to her children is vital to her, her horrified but fascinated evocation of other women's wicked acts shows that she is only with difficulty resisting the desire to emulate them. Once the Nurse begins to push her, she admits that though the fulfilment of her desires is not conducive to honour, it is pleasing to hear (489). Since the Nurse cannot bear to see Phaedra die, she is determined that she should approach Hippolytus, and although Phaedra resists verbally, growing increasingly vehement against 'most shameful words' (499), and though she never actually succumbs to the Nurse, the continual play on words such as 'well' or 'good', meaning 'skilful' or 'expedient', rather than morally upright, underlines her ambivalence. Thus 487 refers to 'words which are too fine', while the Nurse tells her that her advice, though shameful, is 'better' for her than resistance (500), to which Phaedra admits that she speaks shamefully but 'well' (503), and at 505, if she goes on saying such things 'well' (i.e. so persuasively) she will yield. Whether this is a genuine plea to the Nurse to stop, or a subtle admission that she will not fight any more depends on one's general judgement of Phaedra, and is, I think, deliberately left unclear by Euripides. Certainly, by the end of the scene, she has tacitly given up. When the Nurse urges her to let her handle everything, having 'just remembered' that she has some helpful drugs of an unspecified sort, Phaedra fears that she turn out 'too clever', but does not question her too closely. At this point, she is culpable – she could simply kill herself and have done with it – but only a heart of stone (or of Hippolytus) could condemn her outright after her struggles. The Nurse's final appeal to Aphrodite to 'be her fellow worker' (523) is in the circumstances chilling.

Once she is convinced that Hippolytus will reveal her secret, the disastrous effects of her externally-based morality are fully apparent: she will accuse him of rape to hide her own crime. But even when her actions are inexcusable, Euripides rehabilitates her by setting her efforts at behaving well against Hippolytus' complete lack of understanding towards her. The Nurse's intervention obviously removes some blame from her, and even if Phaedra *should* either not have told her or somehow prevented her from approaching Hippolytus, Euripides makes her action understandable, if not excusable. We can pity her because we understand the course of events that led her to act, even while condemning her dishonesty and gross misuse of words relating to morality[8] to justify the unjustifiable.

By the brilliant device of never having the two meet, so that her desire is merely hearsay to Hippolytus, Euripides makes her more sympathetic than would be warranted, because Hippolytus never questions her directly to discover that she is not the stereotypically wanton woman of his prejudices. We have seen her struggles over 500 lines; he has not, and Artemis' convoluted description of her actions as 'wild lust or sort of nobility' (1300-1) sums up her ambiguity. Euripides rehabilitates her by devoting many lines to developing her character and motivation. Explanations for a person's actions tend to create empathy for them, and the reverse is also true. To compare a modern example, in the film *Fatal Attraction*, the day-to-day life of Alex the sex-crazed woman was ignored, so that the dice were loaded in favour of the man whom we saw in the context of his whole life – her craziness was inevitably less sympathetic than his portrayal as a family man. Thus Hippolytus himself has no sympathy for Phaedra when all he sees is her passion, but even he softens a little once he is accused by his father unfairly and, if just a little, begins to understand the anguish of being harshly misjudged (1034-5). Her final threat that 'someone' sharing in her disaster, will 'learn to be virtuous' is born from a complex mixture of fear for her honour, hurt at Hippolytus' cruelty and perhaps anger at rejection.

The Nurse

The prominence of the Nurse's role exemplifies Euripides' tendency to domesticate tragedy and broaden its scope beyond the traditional kings and heroes. If one human character may be held responsible for the tragic events, it is she. Against Phaedra's wishes, she reveals her secret to Hippolytus, and even after this has disastrously backfired, she is still full of schemes for rectifying the situation. From her first entry, in which she complains that Phaedra's illness is making her own life difficult (186), through her immediate desire for suicide at the revelation (354ff.), her philosophy is that since life is painful (189, 207) one should seek an easy life rather than a morally sound but harder one: though she loves Phaedra, at 250ff. she wonders whether human attachment is worth the pain it causes, and espouses a policy of detachment and moderation even in love.

Her claim that nothing in excess is good (261ff.), looks unexceptionable – 'nothing in excess' is an ancient Greek maxim – but she apparently includes moral scruples among the things which should not be taken to excess. She regards morality as not an absolute, but at best something that we can sometimes follow without pain in life's uncertainties. For her, pain must be removed in the most expedient manner possible. Phaedra is in pain because she desires Hippolytus? Then he must be made to reciprocate. She immediately changes her opinions as circumstances dictate: thus at 288, 'Let us forget your previous words', 'Where I said the wrong thing, I will move to a better speech' (296), and 'Second thoughts are best' (435). Painless success is as good as moral action, and her credo is summed up in her self-defence at 700: 'If I had succeeded, then I would have been judged among the wise.'

We are surely not supposed to concur, and yet Hippolytus, whose steadfast adherence to his oath contrasts with her dangerous flexibility, is destroyed by his rigidity and takes several people with him. If he had followed the Nurse's recipe for success, he might have averted much misery. Thus her relativism does have some validity, and it is typical of the shades of grey in this tragedy that a clearly inadequate moral code might both have saved Hippolytus and is based on the time-honoured principle of 'nothing in excess'. Moreover, she is motivated by love for Phaedra, so that love and a desire for moderation, which both look admirable, prove disastrous, as the stronger argument is turned into the weaker once more.

The Nurse applies logic, devoid of moral considerations, to a moral problem. She is an expert at dishonest argument, assuring Phaedra that love (making no distinctions between its objects) is natural. At 445, she even echoes Aphrodite (line 6f.), saying that the goddess is gentle to those who yield to her, but violent to those who 'think big' against her. This is another brilliant example of the ambiguity which is such a feature of this play, because in a sense she is right – if Hippolytus had accepted Aphrodite, Phaedra would not now be dying. Her description of Aphrodite's power and charm is as lyrical and persuasive as Hippolytus' account of Artemis earlier in the play: 'She passes through the sky, she lives in the sea and gives birth to all things, sowing and giving desire' (447ff.; compare the Chorus at 505ff.). And yet, of course, she is arguing for an indefensible act. Her argument that the gods themselves are subject to Aphrodite, so that Phaedra can hardly presume to be better than they, is a classic piece of sophistic false argumentation, and would be recognised as such by the audience.[9] For the realistic Nurse, Phaedra's desire for virtue is foolish because the world is flawed – by contrast, the more idealistic Hippolytus, Theseus and even Phaedra all seek a better world and are disappointed in their hopes.

The linguistic brilliance of the Nurse would do Protagoras proud. Not only is she a glib speaker, but she can even talk Phaedra's language: the wise, she says, should 'hide what is not good' (*lanthanein ta mê kala*, 465-6) echoing (though contrasting with) Phaedra's desire not to be hidden when doing good (*mête lanthanein kala*, 403-4). Mortals should not take excessive care to perfect their lives (*ekponein bion lian*) while Phaedra complains that while we know what is good, we do *not* do it fully enough (*ouk ekponoumen*, 381). The superficial likeness of the language underscores the differences between the two philosophies. Her speech is full of double meanings, enabling Phaedra to interpret it as she wishes: *tolma d'erôsa* (476) can either mean 'endure your love', or 'dare to love'; *tên noson katastrephou* (477) 'master your love' or 'make your love subject to you [i.e. let it do your bidding]'. She recommends incantations and charmed words (478), but will they cure her love or inspire Hippolytus? At 515 she talks of 'joining one delight from two' and while her meaning is ostensibly innocent (referring to preparations for curing Phaedra's love), an alternative meaning is obvious. Yet her trickery is born of concern for Phaedra, who herself recognises the paradox of her ruinous good will, commenting at 597 (cf. 694) that she acted 'kindly but not well'. After her final words at 787, since her function in the play is complete, she is – oddly – seen no more. Some later adaptors of the story pay more attention to realism in their handling of her role at this point.

Hippolytus

Hippolytus alone in the tragedy acts well in human terms, but transgresses fatally in the divine realm. In a particularly ingenious example of the limitations of human knowledge, the catalyst for Phaedra's accusation is his own claim that his mind remained unsworn, when reminded by the Nurse that he had sworn to keep her mistress' secret (612). This, combined with his tirade against women, leads Phaedra to mistrust his words, and to make a pre-emptive strike. Thus he is destroyed – or destroys himself, depending on one's view of his culpability, since the very fact of his death gives rise to two contrary arguments – by words he does not mean, and Phaedra's belief that he does mean them.

Of all the characters in the play, he is the hardest for a modern audience to understand. He tends either to be labelled as 'sexually repressed' or as 'innocent', according to the taste of the critic. Both are misleading. From a Christian background, in which sexuality is often problematic if not actually impure, his aversion may seem less odd to us than it would have done to the average Greek male, of whom Theseus is representative. Since the preservation of the family was of such importance, male celibacy was not generally approved of in Greece, and the necessity of marriage for both men and women (the sex more usually opposed to it) is a theme in a number of Greek myths. Hippolytus is sometimes judged exclusively as a case history of sex-phobia and neurosis, but in fact his attitude to sexuality is just the most striking manifestation of his belief that he is superior to the common herd. The goddess of sexuality punishes him through this particular manifestation of arrogance, but it is more generally his sense of superiority (such as appears in his dealings with the other characters in the play) which is ultimately his downfall. The hero whose arrogance is crushed is a highly traditional tragic character and appears in many different guises: because Hippolytus' particular variant of this plot concerns sex, his character and fate may look more 'modern' than they necessarily are. Contributory to his peculiar character is also, of course, his heritage as the son of an Amazon (10, 351), a race of women known for their hostility to men and thus sexuality.

In E.R. Dodds' formulation, Euripides loves to 'take a one-sided view, a noble half-truth, to exhibit its nobility and then to exhibit the disaster to which it leads its blind adherents – because it is after all only part of the truth'.[10] Hippolytus' life is beautiful and virtuous in many ways, but, like some other Euripidean youths, rigid ideals lead him to reject all forms of ambiguity and compromise. Human piety in a polytheistic world means giving each god his or her due, and this demands compromises that gods themselves need not make. Hippolytus could, and should, revere Artemis while offering Aphrodite sufficient respect to avoid her anger. Such a human compromise would not be the complete capitulation to expediency over morality that the Nurse espouses, but Hippolytus makes no such distinctions. For him it is all or nothing, and in the ambiguity-filled world of the play, human beings cannot make such stark choices and live successfully.

The strange mixture within Hippolytus of the admirable and the peculiar is evident early on. In 58ff. as he brings his garland to Artemis, he sings of the meadow where it had been growing. It is 'pure' (emphatically repeated twice in 4 lines), free from flocks and cultivation, and watered by the goddess Aidôs herself, as a mark of his own reverence. It belongs to those who need no teaching, but who have in their natures virtue (*sôphronein*) in everything always: 'the bad' have no place here. His speech is so beautiful that it is hard at first to realise that it contains hints of the attitude that has incurred Aphrodite's wrath. The meadow symbolises his virginity, detached from human relations and unchanging, but this state is not a permanent option for any human being. Humans must live within society, and to be perfect and unchanging in social relations is impossible. Hippolytus is mistaken to think that he is allowed to be different from others or to regard his meadow as 'pure' because it lacks flocks and cultivation. While places sacred to divinities are often free from normal activity as a mark of their special status, Hippolytus' insistence that only he and his friends are allowed entry conveys the impression that he regards himself as worthy of the special consideration given to a divinity. In fact, he is a human being and agriculture is not impure for humans, but – like sex and marriage – normal and necessary.[11] Thus Euripides hints that the meadow's beauty is excessively rarefied, like Hippolytus' life, and by calling it 'pure' because uncultivated, Hippolytus makes the same mistake as he does in equating alienation from Aphrodite with 'purity' (102). A 'purity' which is dependent on impiety towards Aphrodite is not purity. Emblematic of his detachment from the physical world is his devotion to a goddess whom he can hear but not see.

Indeed, his claims to special purity would have struck an audience as unusual. Purity in regular Greek cult differs from Christian purity, in depending not on interior cleanliness but on avoiding ritual taboos or performing particular ritual actions. Only certain mystery religions demanded a purity based more on attitude than action, and even they were very different from Hippolytus' brand of religion, since they were open to everyone, whereas Hippolytus makes an elitist division of men into the

66

worthy (himself and his friends) and the 'bad' (apparently everyone else). His belief that virtue is innate and unteachable is an aristocratic doctrine which conflicts with contemporary democratic ideals, and indeed with the sophists' claims that virtue is teachable.

This scene shows his life to be beautiful but incomplete, and the subsequent scene shows it to be dangerously narrow. When his old servant urges him to respect Aphrodite, he is rudely dismissive – always a disastrous strategy for human-divine dealings. His sense of entitlement is especially indicated by the series of plays on the word *semnos* and its cognates (93-104). Used 14 times in the play, the word is etymologically connected with *sebomai*, 'I worship', and its meanings run from 'reverend' (cf. 25, 62, 143, 713, 746, 886, 1130) to 'arrogant' (someone who demands to be revered). 'Proud' has a similarly ambiguous sense in English. The servant asks if Hippolytus knows that mortals typically hate pride (*to semnon*). He agrees that they do, and the servant then asks if the same is true among the gods. Hippolytus replies that it is, if gods and men use the same customs. He seems sure that they do, though we have already seen that Aphrodite regards Hippolytus' strivings towards divinity as 'more than mortal', and the end of the play will show just how different divine and human customs really are. The servant then asks (99), 'Why do you not address a *semnê* goddess?' The word must now mean 'reverend', as at 103, where the servant emphasises Aphrodite's importance for men, but it is hard immediately to banish its less flattering connotations. Euripides' word-play leads us to compare Hippolytus' arrogance with that of the goddess he hates as much as she hates him. His rationalisation of his disdain is revealing – 'Different gods and men have different favourites' (104). This, combined with his belief that he is uniquely blessed in his 'companionship more than mortal', indicates that he considers himself to be closer to the gods than other men. He feels *semnos* because he venerates

Artemis so piously (*eusebês*, 83, 656, 1309, 1339, 1368, 1419, 1454; *sebô*, 996, 1061) But the play will show that though gods and men can be *semnos*, they are not held to the same standards. A human being can only be *semnos* in the bad sense of 'arrogant', not the good sense of 'reverend', which is reserved for gods, and any man who strives to be reverend will incur divine punishment. A god can be either 'reverend' or 'arrogant', but even if 'arrogant' she will avoid punishment and will able to have revenge on those 'arrogant' towards her.

Hippolytus' desires are unique among men and uniquely unobtainable. Aphrodite complains from the start that he 'alone' of all the citizens hates her, and her claim is ominously echoed in his rather complacent comment (84) that to him 'alone' is granted the power to 'be with' Artemis.[12] To deny Aphrodite is to deny change and intercourse in all its senses: unlike gods, human beings can avoid neither of these. Thus he appears nervous when Aphrodite is mentioned (100): when the old man persists in his advice, he tries to change the subject and avoids speaking her name until his dismissive parting shot (113), 'I bid many farewells to that Aphrodite of yours.' It is now clear to the audience why he will be punished. The servant's approach to Hippolytus also seems slightly nervous, as if the youth's violence and foolishness frighten him. In an attempt to make Aphrodite less hostile to Hippolytus' impious words, particularly his claim, 'Since I am pure, I greet her from afar' (102), he begs her vainly to forgive his youthful ignorance (117): 'Gods should be wiser than men.'

Hippolytus' arrogance and distaste for the 'works of Aphrodite' are even clearer in his encounter with the Nurse. Since he divides the world into good and bad, with no room for ambiguity, he automatically condemns the Nurse and Phaedra, and does so with unusual violence. The Nurse begs him for forgiveness because to err is human (615), but he ignores her pleas. Whereas Aphrodite will ignore the servant's plea for forgiveness with impunity, Hippolytus' 'godlike' refusal here will ultimately cause his death. Human beings need to forgive one another because they are so vulnerable, and thus, at the end of the play, father and son will forgive one another. By contrast, immortality means never having to say you are sorry, and Artemis and Aphrodite will continue to harm each other unrepentantly.

Though Hippolytus' horror is understandable, 500 lines have focussed on Phaedra's plight, so that his instant and violent denunciation might seem very harsh to an audience. In a long speech, he wishes for a world without the women he so detests. His language is notably violent by the standards of Greek tragedy, as he denies even human status to them, and wishes to lock them up under the guard of beasts. The depth of his misogyny is appalling to modern ears, but misogyny was common in Greek society, and nobody in the play criticises him for it – indeed, the Chorus agree with his own assessment of his excellence. I suspect, however, that Euripides does intend to portray his hatred as excessive, and typical of the extreme behaviour that attracts punishment in tragedy, since lines 664-5 – 'I will never be done with hating women, *not even if someone says I am always going on about it*' – do suggest that he is aware that he may seem obsessed. While the 'clever woman' who sits indoors plotting against men is demonised at least as early as the satirist Semonides (7.70-83), even Semonides admitted that a few good women do exist (7.84-94). There is no parallel in his or any other text for the violence of Hippolytus' sentiments, and his attitude to Aphrodite and all that she represents is likely to have struck the audience as extraordinary in a young man. Most male misogyny is at a much calmer pitch. Although at 656 he reaffirms his intention to keep his oath, and does so, Phaedra is convinced that he will not, and given his earlier denunciation, in another example of the fallibility of human perceptions, it is understandable that she does not believe him.[13]

Hippolytus' scene with Theseus reveals even more of his

disdain for normal human relations. He begins his speech for the defence by claiming that he is bad at speaking to the 'crowd' (a word whose tone is derogatory) since those who are less competent with them are better among the wise – a strange opening to a man who is his king, father and judge! His speech consistently praises his own outstanding virtue (*sôphrosynê*, 995) and alleged purity from sexuality (*hagnon*, 1003, cf. 102). Since his oath prevents him from telling the truth, perhaps he cannot do much more than this, but even so, his tone is unlikely to persuade someone who already interprets his self-praise as hypocrisy. His loneliness is very evident when he argues at cross-purposes with his father in an attempt to prove his innocence. Was Phaedra the most beautiful woman in the world, he asks at 1009, and clearly thinks that the answer is an emphatic no. Since his nature is devoid of human affection, he seems to grasp neither that this response is unlikely to win Theseus' sympathy, nor that his love for Phaedra was not a simple matter of how beautiful she was.

He tries again. Did he want to control Theseus' household and be king? Or is kingship pleasing for those who are sensible (*sôphrôn*, 1013-15)? Of course, his answer is no, and this tactless expression is unlikely to please a king. He says instead that he desires to live with his companions (1016ff.), since the obligations of citizenhood – family, political life, military service – do not interest him. But his choice is not possible. Men must marry, have families and be ready to participate in the affairs of their city: as one of Theseus' potential heirs, he cannot simply refuse all this. Even his patron Artemis is not only the goddess of hunting and virginity, but is also associated with childbirth (166-9) and rearing children to adulthood, while she also presides over the transitions that make the human world run properly. Hippolytus, however, remains fixated with Artemis as hunting goddess and refuses to make his own transition. The cult set up in his memory (1425ff.) is for young women on the

70

brink of marriage: clearly his fate is intended to emphasise that they must make their own transitions from girlhood to womanhood if they are to live successfully.

Does his desire to keep a virtuous reputation make him behave with a foolish rigidity? Breaking an oath is usually wrong, but by doing so, he would have saved himself and others from destruction. To break the oath, however, would be to follow the Nurse's outcome-based morality. Yet in a world where so much that is normally beneficial brings disaster, might it not be better to adopt her beliefs after all? Or is it better for the world as a whole that Hippolytus should have kept his oath, even if in the specific circumstances it caused pain? And certainly, Hippolytus himself says that there is no guarantee that Theseus would have believed him even if he had told the truth (1062-3). Euripides poses a brilliant conundrum. Hippolytus is not a complete innocent, however: he hints several times that he is withholding information, in the expectation that Theseus will be moved to ask questions. At 1032, he says that it is not right for him to 'speak further', and then, as riddlingly as Phaedra trying to steer the Nurse into asking the right questions, 'She was virtuous (*esôphronêse*) not being able to be virtuous (*sôphronein*), while I who could be do not use it properly.' Theseus is too convinced of his guilt to explore this intriguing utterance, and only gradually in their dialogue (1051, 1055, 1070) does it occur to Hippolytus that his father will not be moved. The more he tries to convince him, by repeating the same claims to virtue that he has always made, the more angry Theseus gets at his apparent hypocrisy. At 1060f. he appeals to the gods in another desperate attempt to encourage Theseus to ask questions, but all he says is, 'Ugh, how that high-mindedness[14] of yours will kill me!'

Hippolytus' last two appeals are even less effective. At 1074f. he wishes that the house could bear witness for him, and Theseus sneers that a voiceless witness is the only possible one for him. At 1078 he wishes that he could stand beside himself and weep at his troubles, but Theseus sees only narcissism in his plea – 'How like you to worship (*sebein*) yourself!' The Chorus, of course, know that he is innocent (1103ff.) and the messenger is also on his side, mentioning the crowd of mourners at his departure, but all his admirers (58ff., 1173ff.) are shadowy compared with Theseus or Phaedra, and he lacks the human warmth that is another of Aphrodite's gifts. The messenger concludes his account of Hippolytus' suffering with the loyal assertion that he can never believe in his guilt (1249), and commentators have noted some irony in the fact that both the Chorus of women and a slave champion this aristocratic misogynist.

Hippolytus is convinced of his own virtue, which is often denoted by the word *sôphrosynê* and its cognates. Frequently, he himself claims this quality (e.g. 79, 995, 1007, 1035, 1100, 1364-5, cf. 1013) and he is supported by Artemis at 1402: although Phaedra at 731 and Theseus at 949 both fling his claims back at him in anger or mockery, it is clear that the play associates this word very strongly with him. Like other words in this play, however, it is associated with more than one character and means different things to different people. The word literally means 'safe-mindedness' and has a range of meanings from 'good sense' to 'virtue'. Thus at 704 the Nurse says, '*ouk esôphronoun*' which has a practical, rather than moral meaning[15] – 'I was not sensible' – while the use of the word in connection with Phaedra represents her moral ambiguity. She aspires to *sôphrosynê* (399, cf. 431) and while at 494, the Nurse states that she is not *sôphrôn* in her love (cf. 667), at 358, she is '*sôphrôn* but an unwilling lover of the bad', while Hippolytus' own judgement (1034-5) that Phaedra 'was virtuous not being able to be virtuous' encapsulates the difficulty of summarising her moral position (cf. 1300-1). That the same word is used by and of different characters in so many senses illustrates just how uncertain language and right conduct are in this play.

For a Greek, 'safe-mindedness' depends on self-control, and one specific meaning of *sôphrosynê* is self-control in sexual matters. Hippolytus confuses the two so that what he regards as *sôphrosynê* in its broadest sense (virtue) is at most *sôphrosynê* in its narrow sense (sexual temperance), and since his claim to *sôphrosynê* causes him to regard others as deficient in virtue (667, 1013), it actually contradicts the whole idea of moderation and safe-mindedness. He is far from 'safe-minded' in thinking that his attitude to Aphrodite is virtuous. *Sôphrosynê* is as important to Hippolytus as honour is to Phaedra (e.g. 47, 423, 489, 687, 717). Her honour depends on a reputation for *sôphrosynê*, but just as her honour is ultimately based more on appearance than reality, so his *sôphrosynê* is partial and synonymous only with sexual abstinence. In this desire for virtue combined with a fatal selectivity in its true meaning, they are similar, and thus the use of *sôphrosynê* among other words helps to underline how alike they are.

Even near death, Hippolytus never admits that his conduct is connected with Aphrodite's vengeance. In his lyric lament when he is carried on stage, he complains (naturally) of his unjust father (1348, 1363, 1377f.) but also invokes Zeus to look on the 'proud (*semnos!*) god-worshipper', the man supreme in *sôphrosynê* (1364-5). Artemis agrees with his assessment that his *sôphrosynê* destroyed him (1390, 1402), yet her perspective is that of a goddess who, unlike a human being, is allowed to hate a fellow divinity. Hippolytus resembles his father in his certainty that he is right, and the limited vision of both men is disastrous. The phrase *poll'egô chairein legô* ('I bid many farewells to') is used by Hippolytus dismissing Aphrodite (113) and repeated by Theseus dismissing his pleas to investigate his case further (1059).

73

Theseus

How is it that Theseus kills his son yet is forgiven by Artemis? A partial answer is that Euripides has made his relationship with Phaedra very different from its earlier portrayal. The first play portrays a philanderer who had gone on a dangerous mission to abduct the queen of the underworld. In the second play, he is on a safer and more virtuous journey to an oracle. It is given no particular motivation and is clearly invented to enable his absence when Phaedra falls in love. But this virtuous journey helps to sanitise him, as does his passionate grief at his wife's death. Their apparent mutual devotion makes Aphrodite's meddling all the crueller. Just before Theseus reads Phaedra's letter, he says that he will honour any request she makes that he not remarry (860-1). This is a minor but telling adaptation of tradition, since Theseus was known for a polygamous love life: a Theseus who renounces this element in his traditional persona is devoted indeed!

Theseus' scene with Hippolytus repeats many verbal, thematic and dramaturgic motifs of the rest of the play. Like Hippolytus with the Nurse, Theseus is so angry that he cannot at first speak directly to him (916f.), but makes a general denunciation of hypocrisy that is also directed at Hippolytus. Like his son and wife, he longs for a different world – one in which right conduct could be taught as though it were technical knowledge. But, like Hippolytus (616ff.) and Phaedra (386f.), he wants the impossible, since right conduct and technical knowledge are very different, and both Hippolytus (79f.) and Phaedra (373ff.) deny that it is teachable at all.[16] Theseus' wishes that a man should have two[17] voices, so that whenever he was lying his honest voice would refute him (928ff.) or his suggestion that there will have to be two worlds for the good and for the evil (940ff.), are so fantastical – like Hippolytus' wish for a womanless world – that they emphasise the gulf between the ideal and real worlds that makes this play so tragic.

By having Theseus instantly believe Phaedra, Euripides suggests that he has never entirely trusted his odd son. Similarly, Hippolytus believes unquestioningly in Phaedra's wickedness. Both men behave as though they have somehow been expecting the events to happen and in both cases, in a technique more common in modern novels than in Attic tragedy, Euripides hints at their history outside the immediate tragedy. In particular line 1080, 'You have *always* worshipped (*sebein*) yourself far more than you have behaved justly to your parents', suggests a series of prior misunderstandings between them. In the language of the lawcourts, which underlines how unjust a 'trial' is in which the sole judge asserts the defendant's guilt and only afterwards attempts to prove it, Theseus claims that his son is caught and convicted (944, cf. 955 and 959) of being 'utterly evil' (*kakistos*, 945, 959, as Hippolytus called Aphrodite at 13 and as Artemis will call Theseus at 1316). Since he has already irrevocably cursed him, this trial is a particularly poignant example of the impotence of human language. At 948ff. he flings Hippolytus' own self-praise back at him in mocking irony – are you the proud one (948, cf. 445), do you associate with the gods (*xunei*, cf. 17, 85), are you virtuous (*sôphrôn*) and pure of evil (*kakôn akêratos*, cf. 73, 76)? He accuses him of fake mysticism and hypocritical asceticism[18] and of covering wickedness with high-minded (*semnoi*, 957) words – in fact, he accuses Hippolytus of the same disjunction between outward excellence and inward evil that Hippolytus claims is typical of women. The disjunction between appearance and reality also underlies, and ultimately undermines, the truth of his accusation: first, like Phaedra and Hippolytus, his desire for a good reputation (appearance) leads him to act unwisely (reality), by justifying his curse with an appeal to the heroic reputation he must maintain (977f.). Moreover, although he is wrong about Hippolytus, his arguments are based on apparently clear evidence and his own perceptions of likely motives, even though these appearances are totally false. His words at 971f. (cf. 1057-8) – 'Why do I argue with you when the corpse is lying there as a clear witness?' – are particularly ironic, as is his assertion that Phaedra would not have killed herself out of hatred (962f.) In a sense, that is exactly what she has done! Of course he is wrong, but his motivations for arguing like this are clear.

Yet Euripides makes Theseus more sympathetic by making his son less so. Hippolytus does not help himself by his aloofness and failure to offer Theseus anything other than his usual self-praise. Above all, Euripides' handling of the curse in the extant play makes a great difference to Theseus' portrayal. In the first play, Theseus killed his son with the third of Poseidon's prayers, so that he knew that his curse would work. In the extant play, however, it is the first prayer that he uses and he is less sure of its effect. As soon as he thinks that Hippolytus is guilty, he invokes Poseidon (887f.) but at once (893) adds exile as a human alternative to divine punishment. Thereafter, only exile is mentioned as his punishment (973ff., 1048f.), until the messenger's entry, when he is shocked at his news: 'O gods and Poseidon, so you were my father!' (1169ff.). While he is still culpable, in cursing his son he is not *knowingly* using a method that had been efficacious twice previously, and his response to the news is sober, not triumphant. Moreover, Aphrodite has prophesied that he will do this (43f.), and since he can hardly act otherwise, his guilt is somewhat lessened.

Euripides is masterly at manipulating his audience emotionally. Hippolytus is at his least attractive in his scene with the Nurse, while with Theseus, he is pathetic yet not utterly sympathetic in his inability to understand his father. But once the messenger has described his dreadful fate, as the bull roars up from the Saronic gulf (scene of Theseus' own triumphs, 1200, 1208) so that he loses control of his beloved horses[19] and his chariot is broken, one can only pity him. Once the dying youth is on stage, though he remains convinced of his own virtue, pity supersedes harsher judgements.

Gods and men

The play continually questions the relationship between men and gods. The divinities who appear in person show how wide the gap is between gods and men that Hippolytus wrongly thinks that he has bridged. His 'companionship more than mortal' (19) means not that he is nearer divinity than other men, but that his status is anomalous and temporary, and though he imagines himself as Artemis' friend, she cannot cry for him (1396) or stay to see him die (1437f.), and he never even sees her – when she appears at 1391, he simply smells her divine smell. It is hard to know whether his response to her farewell – 'Easily you leave our long companionship' (*homilian*, 1441)[20] – is resigned or reproachful. Moreover, while he regards her as 'greatest' and Aphrodite as 'worst' (16, 13), this opposition is false. At the start of the play, Aphrodite's appearance is immediately followed by the hymn to Artemis (57-8); at its end, the Chorus' hymn to Aphrodite precedes Artemis' epiphany, and her language echoes that of Aphrodite – 'I will make progress' (*prokopsô*, 1297) echoes line 23, 'having made progress' (*prokopsas*); 'to reveal' (*ekdeixai*, 1298) echoes 'I will reveal' (*deixô*, 42). *Timôrêsomai*, 'I will have revenge' (on Aphrodite's favourite), 1422, is used by Aphrodite at 21 to announce her revenge on Hippolytus. The two are not so very different.

The gods do not forgive one another, and since they can never seriously harm one another, their human favourites become each other's targets in their eternal hostilities (1420ff.). Aphrodite has no pity for her enemy or for those whom she destroys with him: she lacks human warmth and forgiveness because she does not need them. Even Artemis reveals a coldness inher-

ent in divine-human relations, when she explains to her 'friend'
that she could not save him because a god never intervenes in
another god's business – in other words, they respect one another more than any human being (1328-30).[21] Hippolytus'
tragedy is that he tries to behave more like a god than a man,
seeing people in absolute terms as 'good' (to be supported) and
'bad' (to be destroyed), but such absolutes are only appropriate
for Aphrodite (5-6) and Artemis (1339-41). Artemis vows revenge on Aphrodite, but as soon as Hippolytus wishes that he
could curse Aphrodite, she stops him (1416-17). She can say
such things, but a human cannot.

It is natural for the humans at the mercy of divinity both to
hope that its rules of conduct are essentially the same as ours,
so that we can understand the gods and find success by copying
them, but also that beings more powerful than men are also
morally better. As the servant says, 'Gods and men should not
resemble one another in their passions.'[22] But at line 7, Aphrodite had warned that 'among the gods, *too*' there is a desire to
receive respect from others, while Hippolytus' dialogue with the
servant also asserts that gods and men operate in the same way
(91-8), and the play bears out his view. While they are all too
alike in their passions, the gods avoid punishment for behaviour
that destroys human beings, and while they behave as badly as
human beings do, they do not even forgive one another as the
human characters do at the end of the play. Meanwhile, the
human beings who behave like gods, or invoke divine power to
work for them, are destroyed. In this, the gods are thoroughly
traditional, in spite of Euripides' modernism in other ways: the
Aphrodite of the *Hippolytus* behaves like Poseidon in the *Odyssey* who harasses Odysseus relentlessly for daring to blind his
son. Aphrodite's honour has been wounded and her punishment
will be viciously precise – what worse punishment could there
be for someone who hates sexuality than a forced encounter
with incestuous adultery?

78

Yet at the end of the play there is some brightening, as divinity, having wrecked several lives, presides over a human reconciliation, and the power of Aphrodite in her role as goddess of all human contact, not just the sexual, is reasserted in gentler form. The one who had refused contact with others (606, 1086) preferring invisible Artemis, is embraced by Theseus (1431-2, 1445). At 1435, Artemis orders Hippolytus to forgive his father, in accord with Attic law whereby a victim could absolve his killer before his death, so as to free him from punishment, but even before this, at 1409, he says that he laments for Theseus more than for himself. Artemis herself softens towards Theseus and Phaedra – his wicked act can be pardoned (1324), hers was wild lust or sort of nobility (1300) since it is understandable that men should do wrong when the gods intervene (1433-4). After Artemis' acknowledgement that no one except Aphrodite is really to blame, Theseus is finally able to pay full tribute to Hippolytus' virtue (1452, 1454).

The Chorus

The role of the Chorus in the play is typical of Greek tragic choruses. As Trozenian women, their immediate loyalty is to Phaedra, but once she has committed her crime, it is Hippolytus to whom their sympathies are directed. Dramatic convention makes them typically reactive and supportive rather than dominant in the action. They introduce characters (170f.), give information to new arrivals (797ff.) or to the audience where necessary (133ff., 268ff.), comment on speeches (431f.) and their reactions can guide those of the audience and voice the emotions of the other characters (e.g. 362ff.). An omnipresent Chorus creates conflicts between convention and realism: how can they know of Phaedra's misdeeds and not tell Theseus? Euripides solves the problem the usual way, by making them swear not to reveal her plans (713-15). Again, while she is hanging herself, they are not allowed to intervene and must delay in helping her until it is too late (778ff.). Their strictly reactive role means that they can never influence the action, and though they advise Theseus not to believe Phaedra's letter, of course he ignores them (891-2, 900-1).

Their other main function is to lead the audience away from the immediate action with lengthier lyric utterances which offer a different perspective on it. Thus at 525ff. (cf. 1268) they sing of the alarming power of Eros, and hope to be spared Phaedra's experience. They then move into the world of myth, where present is assimilated with past, and we see that such events are not isolated but part of recurring patterns in the universe. Past also shades into future, as the Chorus are granted a poetic and prophetic vision that transcends the present – here, they compare Phaedra's violent experience of love with that of Iole and Semele. Since both were destroyed, this is not a good omen. The sense of foreboding is intensified in their next song at 732ff. just before Theseus returns, in which, in beautiful lyrics full of longing for a better life with the gods, they desire escape from the tragedy. Though they hope that all will be well, they review the disaster that Phaedra's marriage has become and their prophecy that she will hang herself undercuts such hopes.

1104-50 is the *stasimon* most closely tied in with the themes of the play, since it expresses doubt in divine care for us.[23] Though they want to believe in divine goodness, reality proves disappointing, and the conclusion they draw (1115ff.) is interesting – 'May I have an easy disposition, *changing always*, and in this way may I live happily.' Does this conclusion simply reject Hippolytus' excessive rigidity, or does it actively endorse the Nurse's view of life (cf. 261)? Once again, Euripides raises the fundamental question but leaves its answer unclear.

This *stasimon* offers an added problem, since the gender of the Chorus apparently shifts between feminine and masculine, which has led some critics to believe that it is sung in alternate stanzas by the women and an extra male chorus, generally assumed to be that of Hippolytus' companions who sang the hymn to Artemis with him at 58ff. The arguments for and against a second chorus are complex.[24] In favour, Hippolytus' plea to his companions to escort him from the country could certainly be answered by the arrival of this chorus (1098f.), but on the other hand, Hippolytus should leave the stage immediately with his father at 1101 while the chorus of companions – who should be accompanying him (1098f., 1179) – must remain on stage at least until 1130, and probably should not depart until the end of the whole stasimon (1150). This problem has not yet been satisfactorily solved, and there may be other explanations for the stasimon's masculine endings, such as textual corruption.

Language and uncertainty

A tragic hero typically makes some mistake, because he is a man with limited perception, and is destroyed. Euripides explores this typical tragic structure by questioning the relationship between language, perception and reality. His characters consistently act on their perceptions with disastrous results: Phaedra's perception of Hippolytus, Hippolytus' of women, the Nurse's of Hippolytus and Theseus' of his son are all flawed. Arguing from what is likely – as we do every day[25] – proves disastrous in this world where even 'clear' evidence of Phaedra's body is not so. Nobody can obtain reliable knowledge, and their attitudes and aspirations are questioned and often destroyed. Hippolytus is forced to encounter sexuality, in spite of his attempts to avoid it, Phaedra desires to be remembered for nobility but will be eternally remembered for its opposite (1429-30), Theseus the family man loses that family, while the Chorus no longer believe that the gods care for man. The play illustrates both the Nurse's complaint (193ff.) that we are 'borne along by words in vain' and Phaedra's lament that we never know what is clearly in place (386).

Duality and repetition

Phaedra's confusion over the two types of shame represents a general uncertainty about language and meaning. Related to the theme of uncertainty is that of duality (inherent in Euripides' decision to write two Hippolytus plays). Duality itself has a dual aspect, of the linguistic and the visual, in the many repeated or mirror scenes: indeed, reflection in a hall of distorting mirrors is an apt image for the representation of reality in this play. Euripides consistently reverses 'stronger' and 'weaker' arguments, while key words, such as *'semnos'* and *'sôphronein'* mean different things to different characters. The main characters are connected by certain words that are frequently repeated, such as 'I trip up' (*sphallô* – 6, 100, 183, 262, 671, 1232, 1414), 'in vain' (*allôs* – 197, 301, 375-6, 535-7, 1367) and the mass of words concerning the nature of moral conduct, such as reverence (*aidôs* – 78, 244, 335, 385, 998, 1258), honour (41, 423, 489, 687, 717, 1301) and, of course, *sôphrosynê*. The series of plays on *kalôs* ('well') between the Nurse and Phaedra (487f.) shows how easily and disastrously the moral and intellectual dimensions of one word can be confused, and though Phaedra tries at first to choose what is good over what is merely clever, circumstances lead her to misuse moral terminology to justify an immoral decision (717, 719) as shockingly as the Nurse does.

The play is full of verbal and visual repetition. Phaedra is dying at its beginning, Hippolytus at its end. Just as Hippolytus is initially unwilling to mention Aphrodite's name, so Phaedra manipulates the Nurse into saying *his* name, and just as she will not speak directly of her love, so Hippolytus only hints at the truth to Theseus. Phaedra's denunciation of adulterous women (413f.) foreshadows Hippolytus' denunciation of the entire female sex (640.) The Nurse supplicates both Phaedra and Hippolytus, and though one supplication is successful and one an apparent failure, each contributes to the tragedy. Hippolytus falsely accuses Phaedra of wickedness and in his turn is falsely accused by Phaedra and Theseus. Hippolytus' tirade against women directed at Phaedra is echoed by his father's tirade against hypocrisy directed at him. Hippolytus finishes this speech with a wish that someone should teach women to be virtuous (*sôphronein*), while Phaedra's last words are that someone by sharing her troubles will learn to be virtuous (*sôphronein*). As she is about to accuse Hippolytus, she takes the control of the stage that the Nurse had earlier and underlines the parallel between the two scenes verbally: her 'I shall arrange my affairs well' (709), echoes the Nurse at 521. Hippolytus places a garland on Artemis' head; Theseus tears his garland from his head. His wish (1074f.) that the house could speak aloud for him contrasts with Phaedra's dread of the house doing just that (415ff.) Hippolytus' farewell to Artemis among his friends (11178f.) recalls the happier days at 58ff. Artemis uses many words used by Aphrodite. Wishes for a different world abound, and the two worlds – one actual, one imagined – duplicate the duality inherent in Phaedra's wish for two different words for the two types (*dissai*) of *aidôs* or Theseus' that men should have two (*dissas*) voices, in this play of two women, two men, two goddesses.

The *Hippolytus* is an outstandingly complex play in which nothing is what it seems. Even Euripides' reworking of his earlier theme contains a bitter irony – although Phaedra struggles to avoid doing what she did in the earlier play, the play ultimately seems to corroborate Hippolytus' worst fears about the female sex, since she cannot avoid reverting to her traditional role: Aphrodite is not to be escaped.

5

Critical Views of Euripides and Hippolytus

Modern Euripidean criticism begins in the nineteenth century in Germany, where classical literature, especially tragedy, was generally valued for certain characteristics that were considered specifically classical, and any work that did not fit the predetermined model was found to be deficient. For critics such as F. and A.W. Schlegel, whose view ultimately reflects that of Aristotle, tragedy was evolutionary, so that Aeschylus was admired as a pioneer, but it was Sophocles who brought the tragic art to its acme, embodying such quintessentially classical ideals as 'inner agreement and completion' that produces 'peace and satisfaction' in its audiences. Under Euripides, however, tragedy supposedly declined from Sophoclean perfection, and Nietzsche most famously accused him of having caused its death.[1] The tone of extant Sophoclean drama is certainly different from that of much Euripidean drama, and I will begin by citing a few judgements of Euripides, which seem both to represent general perceptions of his work and to indicate why his popularity has fluctuated over the centuries.

The Euripides of Gilbert Murray,[2] in the late nineteenth and early twentieth century, is particularly familiar in English writing. Murray's Euripides was the George Bernard Shaw of his day: modern, an enemy of religion, a feminist, a pacifist and an anti-imperialist whose plays were propaganda for progressive thought. In a similar vein, Arthur Verrall dubbed him a 'rationalist' – a foe of religion – but E.R. Dodds characterised him instead as an irrationalist – one who does not hold that reason alone will always make us good or happy (cf. *Hipp.* 373ff.).[3] This anti-rational element in his work has made him as attractive to late twentieth-century critics as he was unsympathetic to those of the Victorian era. Rationalist or irrationalist? Such opposing judgements are typical of attempts to assess him, and many commentators have noted Euripides' multiplicity of voices and ideas that cannot easily be tied to one particular 'message'. Thus Philip Vellacott[4] characterises him in typical judgements as an able dramatist who suffered from a kind of Aesthetic Attention Deficit Disorder which made him unable to decide whether to produce works of art, to gain popularity, to shock and mystify, or to propagate certain political and social views! David Kovacs, while dissenting from it, offers perhaps the best recent snapshot of standard opinion on Euripides as a sceptic, anti-traditionalist and writer of deliberately contradictory plays which are unconcerned with aesthetic wholeness or organic unity, while Aristotelian notions of responsibility, tragic flaws and heroism are irrelevant to them.[5] In sum, Euripides has often been accused of a certain unevenness caused by an intellectual brilliance which supposedly made him incapable of writing a work in which the individual elements are subordinate to one master conception of what it is 'about'. Only relatively recently have negative judgements arising from critics' sense of the way Euripides *ought* to have written ceded to attempts to understand his work on its own terms.

Paradoxically, however, the *Hippolytus* (along with the *Bacchae*) is often tacitly omitted from such generalisations – especially the unflattering ones – because it does appear to fit a more Sophoclean archetype regarding relationships in the plot between cause and effect and character and action.[6] Moreover, its text may also be deemed 'Sophoclean' in being richer in poetic imagery than other plays of Euripides. Nonetheless, as I attempted to show in Chapter 4, the interest in modern intellectual developments, especially those of sophistic thought, in the protean nature of myth, and in the relationships between the sexes that are so important in Euripidean drama are still fundamental to this play, even though it looks more conventional than many. It is one of those Euripidean paradoxes that Euripides seems to deviate from the Euripidean norms established by critics by having written a play more more apparently regular than many of his others.

Throughout this chapter, I will use the work of individual critics to represent more general trends in scholarship over the past hundred or so years. My account is inevitably partial, and its bias is towards scholarship from English-speaking traditions, since there are so many different approaches to the play, and many areas of interest that have excited critical attention.

There is ample critical literature on the play's origins and antecedents alone. Since there are so many irrecoverable details in the evolution of a myth that we see only at a relatively late stage in its development, some of these studies rely to a large degree on speculation. One of the most reliable, however, is the introduction to Barrett's commentary, which cites useful earlier work on the topic, while Louis Séchan and Hans Herter offer detailed accounts of older French and German discussions of the Hippolytus myth.[7] Material concerning the relationship between first and second *Hippolytus* is especially plentiful, and most writers on the second *Hippolytus* have something to say about the earlier play. Snell, Zintzen and Zwierlein[8] all offer particularly detailed attempts to reconstruct its action, and although they sometimes rely on the unprovable assumption that any material in Seneca and Ovid missing from our *Hippolytus* must reflect the action of the lost play, it is valuable to read them, keeping Barrett's sober presentation of the extant fragments of the first play as a corrective against assuming that we know more than we do. Michael Halleran's excellent edition

of the *Hippolytus* offers a very useful presentation of its relationship to earlier sources and also translates the fragments of
the lost play.[9]

The area of the *Hippolytus* that has generated the most
critical attention is that of characterisation. Older work tends
to assume that his characters are intended to be realistic individuals, and that a close analysis of the text will produce a set
of fully rounded characters such as one might find in a modern
novel.[10] German scholars such as Howald and Zürcher,[11] however, challenged such notions, claiming instead that Euripides
– the unstable playwright again – was interested less in consistent characterisation throughout a play than in achieving
particular effects in individual episodes. Greek dramatic convention occasionally creates instances of characterisation in the
Hippolytus which would jar horribly in much modern drama:
Phaedra is dying at 198ff. but suddenly delivers a highly de-
manding speech at 373ff. Like opera, in which the lungs of the
tubercular can still belt out arias, tragedy is not an entirely
realistic medium. But even Aristotle, whose influential claim
that a drama could lack character but not plot hangs over all
such discussions, admitted that any plot needs characters suf-
ficiently rounded to be credible as the sort of people who would
carry out its action. As I suggested in Chapter 4, the events of
the *Hippolytus* depend especially on character, rather than the
momentum of a plot, because the basic story has been reworked
so extensively. Therefore, although the work of Howald and
others is an important corrective to interpretations which make
insufficient distinction between ancient and modern methods of
characterisation, the portrayal of individual personalities is no
less important to the *Hippolytus* than the structure of its plot.

Each of Sophocles' extant plays contains one dominant character, whose tragic fate comes about through his character and
some mistake or crime that he commits. The structure of the
play depends on the connection between character, actions and

fate. By definition, a tragedy is not a punishment that fits the crime but lies in the disjunction between the mistake made and the disproportionate severity of its punishment. Application of this Sophoclean-Aristotelian paradigm to the *Hippolytus* has been influential. Although Bernard Knox[12] notes that, at least in terms of lines spoken, no individual dominates the play, since Hippolytus speaks 271 lines, Phaedra and Theseus 187 apiece, and the Nurse 216, it is, however, Hippolytus and Phaedra that are its most intriguing figures. Thus, in spite of Knox, much criticism tends to select one or other as the main character and thence certain questions arise which have been answered in surprisingly various ways: if Phaedra is the tragic heroine, what is her mistake and how is it connected with her fate? If Hippolytus, what is his, and how is it connected with his?

Critics do not always assess the pair even-handedly, and George Devereux[13] comments astutely that great works of art are akin to the Rorschach inkblot test, in that what one sees in them is inevitably influenced by one's own psychological make-up. Moreover, Hippolytus himself is so unusual that all judgements on him tend to be highly subjective.[14] My impression is that, overall, Phaedra is admired somewhat at Hippolytus' expense: I myself find it hard to avoid this tendency. Of course, as more perceptive critics point out, behaviour that we find sympathetic or its opposite would not necessarily have been so in ancient Athens. Right conduct had a more external dimension in the Greek world than it does today, so that Hippolytus' self-praise or Phaedra's concern for appearances are not as reprehensible to a fifth-century audience as they are in our culture. Moreover, our heterosexually-oriented world tends to find Phaedra particularly interesting, but for an ancient audience, for whom male relationships would be a more dominant interest, the relationship between Hippolytus and his father, and the maturing process of a young man would have been at least as fascinating.[15]

5. Critical Views of Euripides and Hippolytus

In the prologue, Aphrodite states that Hippolytus' obstinacy against her will cause the tragedy. At first glance, this suggests that he ought not to command unqualified admiration, and this would probably be an uncontroversial interpretation if the play were ascribed to Sophocles. Since this is Euripides, critics doubt that Aphrodite's words can mean something so obvious, and suppose instead that Euripides intends his audience to view Hippolytus as an innocent victim of wicked divinities and thus to condemn the goddess, or even renounce belief in her. It is certainly true that many characters in the play agree with Hippolytus that he is an exceptional human being and only Theseus (on false evidence) condemns him violently, but if the audience is also supposed fully to acquiesce in Hippolytus' opinion of himself, the causal relationship between his fate and Aphrodite's vengeance becomes unclear. There is such an attraction in the transgression-punishment sequence that shapes so much tragedy that I believe one needs to have better grounds for jettisoning it than critics tend to provide.

David Kovacs' account of the *Hippolytus* offers excellent arguments against the common view that treats Phaedra sympathetically at Hippolytus' expense. He regards the assumptions on which much criticism of the play rest as based on Christian, or at earliest, Platonic views of the world. For him, the view that Hippolytus is a smug puritan, so that Phaedra's 'high-minded determination to resist Aphrodite is given excessive credit', is a modern distortion, as are condemnations of Phaedra which criticise her for preferring the appearance of a good reputation to its reality. In Euripidean culture, avoidance of a bad name or acquisition of a good one are acceptable motivations, while self-praise might be simply a matter of truth (Aristotle *Nicomachean Ethics* 1123a). Thus Hippolytus is not conceited, but merely truthful in his claims to a special relationship with Artemis (*Hipp.* 84, cf. 17-19). Kovacs admits that neither Hippolytus' denunciation of Phaedra nor his defence speech to Theseus makes him attractive to modern readers, but regards the misogynistic beliefs that were current in Greece as mitigation. I am sceptical of this for reasons offered in Chapter 4, but more plausible is his suggestion that since Hippolytus is innocent when Theseus accuses him, he should by definition be sympathetic because wrongly accused: moreover, since his honour demands that he must keep his oath of silence, his only defence is a repeated assertion of his virtue. As for the widely-spread condemnation of his 'prudishness', Kovacs points out that such disapproval reacts against the sexual puritanism dominant in the Christian-influenced west, but in places such as Greece where puritanism was never dominant, 'prudishness' will excite mild disapproval at most.[16] As it is, sex is far from a neutral topic even today, and thus vehement reaction against him comes from those hostile to the older puritanism who find Hippolytus' 'sex phobia' abhorrent.

Kovacs offers some excellent correctives to typical judgements, and in particular to simplistic praise of Phaedra or condemnation of Hippolytus, yet he lays insufficient emphasis on two problems. First, the supposedly acceptable protection of her good name motivates Phaedra's unquestionably immoral accusation. Though Kovacs claims that Greek morality condones revenge on an enemy, this is not the moral focus of the play. Phaedra is ultimately forgiven for her actions, but not through appeals to the rightness of revenge, but because of her valiant attempts to resist an irresistible goddess and keep her good name. Secondly, if Hippolytus' chastity is merely a preference to which no one would have objected, why is he killed for exercising it? Is Aphrodite's pettiness really the sole reason? And although Theseus is wrong to believe the false accusation, this is a separate charge from complaints about his son's arrogance which had already more tactfully been made earlier in the play by the servant, whose neutrality is greater than that of Theseus. Although critics often lay especial emphasis on Hippolytus' rejection of sexuality, the problem surely lies in the arrogance of the rejection, an arrogance which permeates all his dealings with others (cf. Chapter 4, p. 65).

Kovacs also suggests that Hippolytus' death is not a punishment as such, because he is a hero like those in Sophoclean tragedy, and as such, different from ordinary people. Heroes are 'unreasonable, deaf to appeal' and unpolitical, and though others urge moderation and reason upon them, they can only be true to their own natures. What happens to a hero is not punishment, because being willing to pay the price of death is proof of true heroism and the hero is ultimately honoured for being different from normal humanity.[17] And yet, it seems hard to separate Hippolytus' agonising death from any concept of punishment, and whatever posthumous rewards he or Sophocles' heroes get, they die because they cannot live in ordinary society: this surely is a punishment. Again, Kovacs argues that Hippolytus is only culpable if he refuses to revere something that he should revere, and since the prologue blurs the distinction between god and man, so that Aphrodite is 'too human' and Hippolytus is 'too divine', he cannot be at fault. Here, I do disagree: since Homer, it is axiomatic that however the gods act, their status is superior and those who challenge their majesty will be punished. Hippolytus' punishment results directly from his irreverence to Aphrodite, and even if one holds that he rises towards the divine while Aphrodite sinks to the human, he is not divine in status, which is what matters. This divine-human hierarchy is ingrained in Greek literature and one must surely assume that a Greek audience would view Hippolytus within it.

Critics like myself, who are sympathetic to Phaedra's struggles, may underestimate the less admirable aspects of her behaviour, but those favouring Hippolytus have no less partial a view. His fans often seem to characterise him as an ordinary youth – awkward, certainly, and with unusual interests, but basically normal, the kind of immature but worthwhile undergraduate that one might encounter in one's university career. As we will see in Chapter 6, recasting Hippolytus in this fashion produces some remarkable adaptations and creative imitations of the story, but it distorts criticism of tragedy in the context of fifth-century Athens. Festugière's description, while extreme, is not untypical: his Hippolytus is a handsome sport-loving type, simple and upright in character, and he comments, 'Like many boys of his years, he has ... a fear, even a certain physical horror, and a scorn, of womankind. There is nothing morbid in his case. He simply does not yet think about love ... All headmasters have known boys of this type.' André Rivier's assessment is equally glowing, while Dimock endorses Hippolytus' view that his chastity is both all-important and identified with a life of perfect beauty and wisdom. At most, he allows that his treatment of others is 'tactless'.[18] Even the more reasonable claim that Hippolytus' response is natural for a virtuous youth faced with incest and adultery[19] seems to me to minimise its violence.

All such assessments make Hippolytus essentially 'normal', though Euripides' interest in unusual psychological states (such as that of the delirious Phaedra at the start of the play) is generally acknowledged. Other critics argue, however, that Hippolytus is unusual by Greek standards, and are often unable to resist speculation on why this is so. This psychological fascination is itself an interesting deviation from the general tendency, especially among more traditional classicists, to avoid any hint of a 'How many children did Lady Macbeth have?' type of criticism, and is itself indicative of Hippolytus' strange character.

Two main methods of 'explaining' Hippolytus stand out in critical literature: one relies primarily on Euripides' text and related ancient narratives; the other elucidates Euripides by more extensive reference to modern theories. The former type of explanation can shade into the latter. Of the former, since Hippolytus is the son of an Amazon – a race of women usually hostile to sexuality – he can therefore be thought to have inherited his mother's nature.[20] Similarly, Roisman and Strauss claim that Theseus' own sexual history influences his assessment of his son's credibility regarding Phaedra's rape.[21] There is both textual (967f.) and mythological evidence for the assumption. Because Theseus himself has been married twice, and Aphrodite's sphere of influence is well-known to him, it is natural that, faced with misleading evidence, he doubts his son's protestations of chastity. Other critics also connect Hippolytus' concern with purity with his status as Theseus' bastard son, although these explanations sometimes shade into mere speculation without apparent basis in the text: for example, Grube suggests that because Hippolytus has been abandoned by Theseus and is ashamed of his mother, he cultivates aloofness and hatred of the goddess who represents his troubles.[22] If so, Euripides could surely have made such motivations more explicit in his scene with Theseus: generally, Greek tragic texts do not demand such an extensive use of imagination for their elucidation.

Since sex and psychology are perennially fascinating to us, it is not surprising that a Greek tragic character whose peculiarities seem to be in the sexual sphere has even been a subject for psychoanalysis.[23] Such scholars find variously that his devotion to the unthreatening virginal goddess Artemis manifests a repressed Oedipal fear of his father, or that he is a narcissist, whose misogyny and focus on purity are ego-compensation devices connected with his illegitimacy, and designed to allay feelings of inferiority. When one considers the constraints laid on Euripides by Greek tragic convention, it seems remarkable that even through the broad brush strokes of ancient characterisation, he has created a character psychologically realistic enough to be analysed thus. Whether or not one is convinced, or accepts the validity of interpreting Greek tragedy through this filter, must be left up to the individual. Critics especially in

England are typically hostile to interpretations of Greek tragedy which treat its protagonists as case studies. John Gould
offers sensible criticism of attempts to link Hippolytus and
Freud and argues that his bastardy is important to the play, but
only because it makes his position in Trozen weak, not for any
more complex reason.[24]

The boldest recent interpretation of Hippolytus is by Hanna
Roisman in the aptly-entitled *Nothing is What it Seems*, which
mingles the anti-puritan and psychological strains of criticism.
By minimising the effect of dramatic convention on what the
characters are made to say, so as to interpret the text as though
it were a series of literal conversations, Roisman claims that
neither character's words can be trusted, since Phaedra entirely
belies her virtuous exterior, while Hippolytus is not as sexless
as he alleges: to give a representative example of her method,
Hippolytus' emphasis on marriage in his tirade against women
suggests to her that he considers marriage as possible for
himself, while his claim (*Hipp.* 1004-5) that he knows nothing
of sex except what he has seen in pictures suggests to Roisman
that sex is not as abhorrent to him as most commentators
assume.[25] I find her interpretations unconvincing for their failure to acknowledge ancient literary conventions, but her book
is stimulating, if only for disagreement. Not too dissimilar is the
methodology of Elizabeth Craik who suggests, through a close
reading of the text, that there is a strongly erotic charge in
much of Hippolytus' language and – less convincingly, given
Aphrodite's complaint that he has no interest in sex of any kind
– that his sexuality is of an effeminate and homosexual type.[26]

Craik's charge of effeminacy is taken up in a different form
by those who place his peculiarities as a Greek male in an
ancient Greek context, using insights derived from the structuralist theory that has been extremely influential in analysing
Greek tragedy.[27] Such critics note that his concern with virginity is more typical of women than of men, and his devotion is

offered to a divinity whose concerns are female.[28] He is also an unusual man in rejecting the public life of the city. Moreover, as Zeitlin notes, the state of virginity should be temporary, prior to accepting adulthood and marriage: Hippolytus might desire to remain a virgin, but the Greek world neither allows him to nor approves of the desire.[29] Robin Mitchell-Boyask[30] characterises Hippolytus as an ephebe or adolescent boy who fails to make the transition to manhood, and interprets his character in a context of Greek initiatory customs, which, among other things, affirm a strict division among boys and girls at adolescence. Mitchell-Boyask argues that since Hippolytus' attachment to the female goddess Artemis signals his refusal to allow his social status to match his biological one, his difference is too unsettling for the community to tolerate it, and thus he is destroyed.

Hippolytus is a strange character. Phaedra is as compelling, but less essentially peculiar, and her motivations are clearer. Judgments of her typically depend on the nature of the relationship between psychological realism and the conventions of Greek tragic dialogue that individual critics see. Critics unsympathetic to her[31] strongly emphasise the disjunction implicit in her speech between the concern for virtue and for its appearance, and lay great weight on the undoubted ambiguities in what she says, both in her 'mad scene' and when she allows the Nurse to handle her affairs. Since Phaedra's mad words are opaque to the Nurse and Chorus but clear to us, such scholars assert that she is not as mad as she pretends, and that she deliberately reveals her love so as to make the Nurse her accomplice in seducing Hippolytus. From this basis, Phaedra's change in mood between 165ff. and 373ff. is interpreted as proof that her former weakness was partly fabricated. There are, however, good dramatic reasons why her words are unclear to the other characters but clear to us, and to assume something more Machiavellian rests on the assumptions both that ancient dramatic characterisation differs little from modern naturalistic techniques, and that ancient dramatic dialogue is never shaped by literary conventions. Her sudden change in behaviour from 165ff. to 373ff. has many parallels in tragedy, and may be compared with the change in Medea between 96ff. and 214ff. of Euripides' *Medea*. Undoubtedly more ambiguous, however, are her exchanges with the Nurse after her initial bout of delirium (311ff.), since her language is highly equivocal. She can neither be silent about her love, nor reveal it. She therefore characterises the revelation that will cause the tragedy in glowing moral terms of the necessity of yielding to a suppliant. This is obviously grist for the mill of her detractors, and Winnington Ingram and Dodds suggest that she abuses admirable principles concerning supplication in order to gratify less admirable urges.[32] Her detractors accuse her of a cynical attempt to gratify her desires while retaining a virtuous reputation; those who are more sympathetic accept the face value of her words, while allowing that they contain an element of unconscious desire. Similar questions apply to the end of the scene: is she so exhausted that she cannot be expected to resist the Nurse any more, or is she blameworthy for deliberately refusing to challenge her? It seems clear that she does suspect that the Nurse is planning some intervention with Hippolytus,[33] but how one interprets her reasons for abandoning resistance will depend on the unclear division between realism and dramatic convention, as well as on prior judgements about her character. Of course, great emphasis has been laid by her detractors on her admission at 403-4. Even if external appearance is important in Greek morality, it is clear that doing right is not synonymous with being seen to do right, and given that this desire leads to the false accusation that she hopes will make her look virtuous and Hippolytus look wicked, it is certainly possible to see a Phaedra without many redeeming features, rather than one who is gradually backed into a corner.

The passage that has generated the lengthiest critical discussion and the least consensus is Phaedra's great speech at 373ff. Many questions surround both the Greek and its meaning in the broader context of the play. Phaedra says that human beings know what to do but do not always do it, but what connection her words have with her plight, whether or not she is including herself in the analysis, and the specific factors in human life which militate against moral conduct are much in doubt. Moreover, since her claim directly contradicts the 'Socratic paradox' that nobody does wrong willingly, some critics suggest that Euripides is directly contradicting Socrates.[34] Others argue that the reference is not specific enough,[35] but whether or not Socrates is invoked here, Euripides, as is his habit, is certainly exploring contemporary philosophy and ethical questions via his tragic characters.

Phaedra says that though we know what right conduct[36] is, we do not act accordingly, but the problems start when she goes on to cite specific distractions from the good, and in particular, whatever it is that is of 'two kinds, one not bad, the other the ruin of houses'. The previous chapter offered my own interpretation of this difficult passage, and it remains to summarise some trends in scholarly opinions on its interpretation, leaving readers to explore the ever-growing literature on the subject. There is a division between those who view it within the context of the whole play and those who restrict its reference to its immediate context. Thus when Phaedra mentions her studies of how human beings fail to reach perfection, critical opinion divides between those who think that she regards herself as one who has already failed to do what she knows to be right (with the implication that she is aware of the potential consequences of her confession), and those who interpret her words as a confident statement that she will succeed where most people fail.[37] Both interpretations have some attraction: the first because Phaedra admits failure in her first two resolutions (*Hipp.* 393-99); the second because this speech is partly intended to reassure her household that she will not disgrace them. (On my interpretation, which follows the second of these, 373ff. would spring from Phaedra's own evaluation of her conduct, according to which she is doing the best she can, by committing suicide, while knowing that she is incapable of abjuring her feelings for Hippolytus, which would be the best thing.)

We go astray, says Phaedra, not because of our intellectual perceptions, since plenty of people have sufficient intellectual capacity, but something between theoretical knowledge of the right and its accomplishment intervenes to cause disaster. What is it? Two translations are plausible. Either, 'Some from laziness, others putting something else, namely pleasure, before what is good', in which case what is good is opposed to things such as laziness and pleasure which are both preferred to it.[38] Or, 'Some from laziness, others putting some other pleasure before what is good', so that Phaedra regards what is good as a positive pleasure in competition with other pleasures.[39] By contrast, the former interpretation offers a Phaedra for whom the good is not so attractive and even a potential hindrance to pleasure. Those who believe in the sincerity of Phaedra's protestations of virtue will therefore prefer the second interpretation: the more sceptical will prefer the first.

Her next lines are the most disputed of all. 'There are many pleasures in life – long talks and leisure, a pleasant evil, and *aidôs* ('shame'). They are of two kinds, one not bad, the other, the ruin of houses (*dissai d'eisin, hê men ou kakê, hê d'achthos oikôn*).' Two translations are again possible: either *aidôs* is itself a pleasure,[40] or it is like pleasure in hindering good conduct, but not an actual pleasure.[41] The linguistic arguments are complex, and demand reading in their entirety, but I am convinced by those who hold that the word order and the Greek word *te* which links *aidôs* to the previous line should indicate that it is one of the pleasures preferred to what is good, although it is certainly a strange pleasure. But whether shame itself hinders the good or whether it is a subset of the pleasures which do so, the discontinuity between it and the good is clear: shame will not always engender right action.

The second major question is whether it is shame or pleasure that is of two kinds. Various linguistic arguments for taking 'two types' (*dissai*) with 'pleasures' have been offered,[42] the strongest of which is that *aidôs* has no plural, and that if Euripides had intended to speak of a double *aidos* he would have made it clear by writing *dissê*, the singular of *dissai*. Moreover, at first sight, it is certainly easier to understand that 'Pleasures keep us from what is doing good: there are two sorts; one not bad, the other, the ruin of houses.' I argue for a different interpretation in the previous chapter, but I acknowledge that it is not undisputed and point readers to other views here, since I am considerably simplifying critical positions which need a careful reading.

The alternative interpretation, that there are two sorts of pleasurable *aidôs*, one good, one bad, is ostensibly harder, but many scholars reluctantly support it on linguistic grounds. It is clear that the good *aidôs* prohibits wrong-doing, but there is no consensus on what the *aidôs* that destroys houses could be. How could an emotion which generally inhibits wrong-doing ever be a pleasure which is both a 'burden on the house' and prevents us from doing what we should?

Interpreters generally explain certain aspects of their presentation of *aidôs* very well, yet fail to account for all of them satisfactorily. There is some consensus that the word concerns one's relations with others, and specifically other people's opinions of one's actions.[43] Several commentators also note that it is traditionally ambivalent.[44] In his now fragmentary tragedy *Erechtheus* (fragment 365), Euripides himself confessed bafflement: 'About *aidôs*, I cannot decide; it is necessary and yet it is a great evil.' Hesiod (*Works and Days* 317-19) says that *aidôs* can help or hinder a man, in that it can prevent him from doing wrong but can also inhibit him from taking any action at all.[45]

If the good *aidôs* beneficially inhibits conduct that others may condemn, its bad counterpart ought to concern paying attention to others in a way which both causes bad decisions about conduct, and which is also pleasurable. It would therefore refer to the desire of Phaedra for a good reputation which is central to her character as portrayed by Euripides. In the play as a whole, it is precisely this concern with reputation that leads her to accuse Hippolytus falsely, and commentators, whether explicitly or implicitly, often take her words on *aidôs* here as a commentary on the whole play.[46] And yet, one must wonder whether at this early point, she could be so clairvoyant about her fate, especially in the light of her strong determination at 401f. to avoid danger by killing herself. Similar doubts must also arise concerning interpretations which connect the bad *aidôs* with her confession to the Nurse, because these also assume that she must know at once that she has set disaster in motion. Such interpretations include that of E.R. Dodds,[47] which has been influential and attractive by being grounded in Euripides' text, according to which the good *aidôs* initially compels Phaedra to be silent about her love (*Hipp.* 244), while the bad (pleasurable) *aidôs* compels her to accept the Nurse's supplication (335) and reveal all. This *aidôs* destroys houses because her confession leads to the tragedy. On related lines, Kawashima[48] argues that there is an innate contradiction between Phaedra's desire for virtue and her plight: either she hides her feelings, so that nobody knows her virtue in trying to suppress them, or she reveals all and seems no longer virtuous. Thus her bad *aidôs* would be the impulse that prompts her revelation.

Another set of interpretations connects Phaedra's words on *aidôs* with the context of her life as an aristocratic woman, in view of 383-4's list of pleasures which are those of a wealthy woman with too much time on her hands. Thus Douglas Cairns relates her *aidôs* to the secluded lives of aristocratic women, in which destructive passions can arise,[49] while Craik goes even further and suggests that *aidôs* is a euphemism for sex.[50] All such interpretations ascribe considerable self-knowledge and a degree of clairvoyance to Phaedra, and make her somewhat complicit in her fate. By contrast, Kovacs interprets the speech more specifically in the context of lines 1-372 by suggesting that she is not apologising for wrong-doing but explaining why she must die: I have suggested above (p. 58) why this is attractive. Since no interpretation of this passage has ever commanded absolute assent, some critics suspect textual corruption, and Sommerstein and Kovacs offer possible emendations.[51] After all this, one can only agree with Phaedra that if 'what is proper' were clear, there would be a linguistic distinction between the good and bad *aidôs* (*Hipp.* 386-7), but whatever its actual nature, the ambiguity of *aidôs* recalls the many other ambiguities in the play that lead to wrong action when right action is being attempted.

Although many critics tend to take sides with Hippolytus or Phaedra against the other, others explore the similarities between them. Some offer an Aristotelian interpretation under which Hippolytus and Phaedra are opposites, exemplifying vices at either end of a virtuous mean that neither achieves. Thus Barnes and Gregory[52] characterise the play as a study in *sôphrosynê* in which both are similarly lacking, as Phaedra is excessively concerned with her reputation, while Hippolytus is obsessed with his chastity and sense of his own rightness. Both are self-conscious and desire public affirmation of their goodness, but neither succeed, since their obsessions lead them to privilege appearance over reality, and their own narrow sphere of knowledge over broader considerations, thereby causing their own destruction.[53] Frischer conceptualises their relationship as 'concordia discors', 'dissonant harmony', in that their characters are ostensibly opposites, yet similar, as revealed by certain visual or verbal clues: thus Phaedra's feebleness at 198ff. is mirrored by Hippolytus' death scene (1347ff., esp. 1361), while there are frequent verbal echoes between the two (compare 399 with 995, 1013 and 1160; 728f. with 667).[54]

The two goddesses are also alike yet opposites, and another major area of critical interest has been the relationship between divine and human in the play, especially Euripides' attitude to the divine presence which frames the human action. These issues, too, influence assessments of Phaedra, since what one believes the cause of her love to be – an actual god or her own sexuality symbolically embodied in the god – will influence assessments of her. Here, a division emerges between more literal conceptions of the gods and allegorical or symbolic inter-pretations, so that some critics minimise the divine action entirely, domesticating and humanising the tragedy, while oth-ers regard the gods as merely anthropomorphised symbols of natural or psychological forces in the human world.[55] Aphrodite becomes sexual passion (or, more broadly, the human impulse for contact),[56] Poseidon and his bull, either the sea or the repressed sexuality that bursts forth to destroy Hippolytus. There is undeniable attraction in this. The idea that the gods really 'stand for' elements in the human world is ancient and contains some obvious truth. Inherent in Greek religion is divinity's double aspect as both person and force.[57] Euripides himself has largely restricted the gods to a framework spanning the human action, which might suggest that he himself consid-ered them more symbolic of human motivations than actual personalities. However, problems arise from simplifying divin-ity in the *Hippolytus* to make it is *exclusively* symbolic. It is not clear, for example, exactly what Artemis, as she is seen in the play, could *symbolise*. Hippolytus' devotion to her ought not to be just a metaphorical way to say, 'Hippolytus is sexually re-pressed', because Euripides has put too much detail into their relationship to boil it down so simply. Again, if Poseidon symbol-ises the sea, how could Theseus ask for and receive a tidal wave in order to destroy his son? If the wave is just an accident, then the story is meaningless. If the bull symbolises Hippolytus' repressed sexuality, how could it actually kill him? How could Theseus be the one to instigate it?

Aphrodite's prologue states that Phaedra has hitherto been honourable, but she has made her fall in love with Hippolytus to be her instrument of revenge on him. A literal interpretation of her words necessitates the belief firstly that her love is involuntary, and secondly, that the goddess of love is petty and will directly intervene in human lives, denying us free will. Some critics are uncomfortable with such premises, and posit that Phaedra's responsibility for her fate must really be greater. Psychology sometimes comes to the rescue, so that some older commentators suggest that the large age gap between Theseus and his wife leads her to look elsewhere for satisfaction,[58] but textual evidence for this view is lacking. More directly grounded in Euripidean drama are suggestions that Phaedra's Cretan connections are more than incidental to the plot.[59] Crete had a reputation, especially in Athens, for being strange and somewhat different from mainland Greece, as the land of labyrinths, Minotaurs and sexual irregularity. The story of the Minotaur, born from the liaison of Phaedra's mother Pasiphae with a bull, was one of the best known of all Greek myths: indeed, Theseus had first met Phaedra and her sister Ariadne on his visit to Crete to kill it. Euripides' play, the *Cretans*, had dramatised Pasiphae's tauric passions. Phaedra herself alludes to the tale (*Hipp.* 337ff.) and regards herself as typical of her family in experiencing a forbidden love. Her leisured environment is also sometimes seen as a contributing factor to her passion. Such theories have some plausibility, because they are compatible with what we know of contemporary mythical and dramatic traditions, whereas more psychologically-based theories are more problematic because they have no ancient basis.

Even if human character is regarded as the prime mover in

the play, human action is framed by one divinity (Aphrodite) who claims that she is responsible for it and another (Artemis) who explains the tragedy as an inevitable result of divine intervention in human affairs. These assertions have been so unpalatable to some critics that they assume that Euripides is satirising traditional myth, so that the audience, or at least an intelligent minority, would renounce belief in it. The idea of Euripides the proselytising atheist has a lengthy pedigree which goes at least back to Aristophanes. Arthur Verrall was its most ardent modern proponent, and Greenwood uses a Verrallian perspective to explain the treatment of the gods in the *Hippolytus*.[60] For Greenwood, the plays are fantasies, and say nothing credible about the gods. He rejects even the idea that Euripides' gods are symbols, because they are actively evil, and he claims that symbolic gods ought, like impersonal forces of nature, to be merely pitiless, not actually nasty. Most other critics are less extreme, but quite a number either deny that Euripides' plot can be taken completely at face value or hold, like Winnington-Ingram, that the explanations given by the goddesses are too 'thin and over-simple' to explain the complexities of human life.[61]

Conacher's view of the gods is intermediate between symbolic and actively sceptical, since he explains the events of the play through human motivations, excluding all divine intervention. For him, Artemis and Aphrodite are forces within the souls of men, but he also notes that their role in the action is highly prominent. Thus he tries to combine symbolic and literal by suggesting that Euripides was 'casting doubt on the less credible features of a myth by *an exaggerated emphasis* [my italics] upon them' in an allegedly 'neo-Homeric primitivism' so crude that his audience could not literally believe in it.[62] For Dodds,[63] too, a more literal interpretation of the play creates not a goddess but a 'petty fiend', so that for him, Aphrodite is an eternal cosmic power – as the Nurse says, something 'bigger than a goddess' – and Artemis is the rather vaguer 'principle of refusal'. I wonder, however, whether one can assume that a fifth-century audience seeing Aphrodite apparently incarnate on stage would interpret her as primarily symbolic.[64] Moreover, since any reader of Homer could easily find examples of divine pettiness,[65] Dodds' assumptions seem a little generous.

Even at a simple practical level, the action only works in a framework of interventionist divinities. If the events of the play – especially Poseidon's role – are not divinely influenced, they become less, not more, credible, by being more coincidental. Thus I am more in sympathy with criticism which makes the gods central to the action,[66] even though it raises serious questions as to whether or not human beings have any sort of free will in such a world. Knox analyses the characters in terms of their choices between silence and speech, and explains how their vacillations create the impression that they do have free will, even though it is entirely illusory: in no other play do characters change their mind so often. Kovacs[67] aptly characterises such divine-human relations as a Grand Master playing chess with a novice – the novice can move as he wants, but the Grand Master is cleverer and can see further ahead. And just as a Grand Master will add insult to injury by naming the exact piece with which he will check mate, so the gods prophesy unavoidable disaster. It is a remarkable tribute to Euripides's creative ability that such diverse interpretations of such a central part of the play have been formulated, especially since there is much plausibility in so many of them. The symbolic and psychological readings do retain an element of attraction, and perhaps one must ultimately allow that the play may be interpreted in several ways which are not always absolutely consistent with one another.[68]

A final distinction may be made between schools of criticism, such as many of the foregoing, that read the play essentially as a story about characters called Hippolytus and Phaedra, and those which consider its action in a more abstract sense, in terms of larger issues of importance in fifth-century Athens that are illustrated by the characters. For example, some critics read the play through a strongly politicised filter, which sets the aristocrats Phaedra and Hippolytus against the democratic Nurse.[69] The desire of Phaedra and Hippolytus for public recognition characterises a quintessentially aristocratic concern with outward appearance. Phaedra's version of the aristocratic code is, of course, flawed, and even Hippolytus' does not bring him salvation in the Euripidean world in which what seems is not what is. By contrast, the Nurse represents a (flawed) version of a democratic-sophistic point of view, in which nothing in the world is fixed or sure, so that we must adapt continually to circumstances.

Gregory argues that rejection of Aphrodite is an anti-democratic act, since the influence she has over all creatures makes her the most democratic god of all, and connects this with Hippolytus' *sôphrosynê*, which is predicated not only on chastity, but also on his belief that he is generally better than other men by differing from them, whether in rejecting sexual contact or political engagement (1016ff.). She then traces the development of *sôphrosynê* from its origin as an ideal that transcended particular political affiliations, to its specific association in the fifth century with oligarchs, who were unsympathetic to the democracy. Since Euripides gives Hippolytus some distinctly oligarchic traits, especially his claims to excellence, disdain for the 'crowd', and lack of interest in political affairs, Gregory suggests that he is emblematic of upper class, anti-democratic Athenians, and, given the fate that overtakes him, suggests that Euripides is urging that *sôphrosynê* be reclaimed from the oligarchs and made a common ideal again.[70]

Another set of interpreters analyse the play in terms of even more abstract oppositions between speech and silence, knowledge and ignorance, or appearance and reality. Deducing hidden causes and invisible truths lying behind surface phenomena of the world was important in the fifth-century speculations, and the conflict between inner truth and outward appearances, and the resulting lack of clarity in the world, where even autopsy is unreliable, is one of the play's most pervasive themes.[71]

The *Hippolytus* contains a richer variety of imagery and verbal play than is usual for Euripides. The complex and lush imagery of Hippolytus' first speech sets the tone for the rest of the play. Moreover, words such as '*sôphrôn*', '*aidôs*' and others are repeatedly used with different meanings and different contexts which help to characterise and make connections between those who use them. Many commentators also show that the use of repeated imagery centring on the sea, water, horses, bulls, knots, yokes and so on is more than mere decoration, and is connected with fundamental themes of the play.[72]

Aristophanes frequently accuses Euripides of misogyny in his unsparing portrayals of female wickedness, although it is as frequently noticed by later critics that even women like Phaedra who act wickedly do so in circumstances that make their deeds understandable, if not justifiable – hence the image of Euripides as feminist. Murray and Lucas[73] suggest that the ambiguity arises from ancient expectations that women should not have any character at all. Since Euripides dramatises old myths which are inherently misogynistic, and gives his women intelligence and personality, it is not surprising that he can be interpreted as a misogynist. Phaedra is a typically ambiguous Euripidean women. Ultimately, she does what the myth dictates, so that she does not escape the role of the destructive woman. On the other hand, Euripides portrays her sympathetically, and since the play twists 'the stronger argument' into the weaker, one can conceptualise its plot either as 'Phaedra destroyed an innocent man' or 'Phaedra was the instrument of Aphrodite when she destroyed an enemy'.[74]

Like all Greek tragedy, the *Hippolytus* has inspired a vast

107

quantity of secondary literature that seeks to explain and interpret Euripides' words definitively. Like all tragedy, it is so
complex that for every statement made, someone else has suggested exactly the opposite. What I have discussed represents a
fraction of criticism on the *Hippolytus*, but I hope that it will at
least be an introduction to some of the issues that have been
considered particularly important in interpreting this play over
the last century or so.

6

The Afterlife of Hippolytus[1]

… Yes, I should like poor honourable simple sweet prim Phèdre
To be happy. One would have to be pretty simple
To be happy with a prig like Hippolytus
But she was simple. I think it might have been a go,
If I were writing the story
I should have made it a go.

Stevie Smith, *Phèdre*

Euripides is quoted more often in later classical literature than anyone other than Homer and Menander. From his fourth-century revival onwards, his influence was immense, and although Plato disapproved of him (*Republic* 568A), Aristotle called him 'the most tragic of poets' and significantly, 'The Euripides-Worshipper' was the title of two (now lost) comedies. 240 BC saw the first adaptation of Greek tragedy at Rome. Of the plays of the main Roman republican dramatists, seven are based on Aeschylus, 16 on Sophocles and 24 on Euripides. It is thus not surprising that Euripides starts to replace Homer as a subject for Graeco-Roman art, and scenes from the Hippolytus story appear frequently on Roman sarcophagi down to the fifth century AD.[2]

Euripides' influence on most Augustan literature was less direct, although Virgil's scorned and vengeful Dido clearly has antecedents in Phaedra and other Euripidean heroines, and Ovid used the story in *Heroides* 4. It was, however, Seneca's *Phaedra* that really ensured the story's longevity in European tradition. Although the acknowledged excellence of Euripides' play meant that it was read throughout late antiquity, as progressively fewer people learned Greek, Seneca's Latin version inevitably came to be favoured over Euripides'. Even when Greek was revived in the Renaissance and the first printed editions of Euripides were produced at the very end of the fifteenth century, although Euripides was translated into French (Tissard, 1507) and Latin (by Martirano, Bishop of Cosenza, 1556), Seneca retained popularity for another couple of centuries. Pomponius Laetus revived his *Phaedra* at Rome in 1490, and English Elizabethan drama shows some Senecan influence. Not until the seventeenth century is Euripides more admired, although his influence on 'stock parts' in Shakespearean drama is sometimes argued: the Nurse in the *Hippolytus* is distantly related via Seneca to Juliet's nurse, as are the confidantes popular on the French classic stage. After Jacobean tragedy, little interest remains in Seneca, and although there has been some revival in modern times, nobody would now consider him a superior tragedian to Euripides.

When one considers the remarkable variety of versions of the Hippolytus story, the singularity of the extant play becomes evident. One reason for this is the influence of Seneca's *Phaedra* on European tradition. Another is that the Hippolytus of the extant play is so unusual that many subsequent adaptations opt for a more conventional character. We saw in Chapter 5 that his celibacy and the role of the gods in the play elicited particularly conflicting responses among critics. It is precisely these two elements that tend to be omitted or substantially reworked in later versions of the story.

Perhaps because the original myth seems fundamentally unfair to Hippolytus, at least as early as Virgil (*Aeneid* 7.761ff.; cf. Ovid *Metamorphoses* 15.541-6, *Fasti* 6.733-56), but probably earlier, he is resurrected as Virbius ('twice man') by Asclepius at Artemis' request, though Asclepius is punished for meddling

110

with fate by being blasted by Zeus' thunderbolt. Hippolytus-Virbius dwells in the Italian woods, where he marries and has a son by a nymph called Aricia. Hippolytus' sweetheart – a role nonsensical in Euripides' *Hippolytus* – will have a particularly long and varied career in European literature.

Ovid's *Heroides* contain our first surviving Roman account of Hippolytus and Phaedra. The *Heroides* is a series of poems written as letters between famous mythological lovers, and poem 4 is a love-letter from Phaedra to Hippolytus. This Phaedra is more akin to Euripides' Nurse, and seems to have few moral scruples about her love, hinting (35-6) that the gods too have irregular affairs, while at 133-5 she justifies incest by citing Jupiter and Juno's marriage. She even suggests that he should usurp the throne (121ff., a detail which may reflect the first *Hippolytus*). Like Euripides, Ovid refers Phaedra's passions to her heredity (53ff.; cf. E. *Hipp.* 337f.) As is common in treatments of the story other than that of the extant *Hippolytus*, Theseus is an unattractive character, here charged both with faithlessness in his abandonment of Phaedra's sister Ariadne on Naxos, and violence in killing not only Hippolytus' Amazon mother (as Seneca also implies) but also her 'brother', the Minotaur (115). Euripides' first play also made Phaedra reproach Theseus for his shortcomings, but tragedy naturally avoids the grotesque idea that Phaedra is the half-sister of a half-bull. Ovid tells the story in his trademark witty style, and adds his own touches, notably in his ingenious suggestion that Theseus finds his friend Peirithous more attractive than Phaedra. The last 40 lines are pure Ovid as Phaedra describes a scene straight out of his *Art of Love* in which she imagines how they could conduct an affair: since they are kin, arranging meetings will be easy, and they will even be praised for filial love (137ff.)! Euripides' tragedy has been transformed into a funny and clever romp.

Although Senecan tragedy is outwardly traditional in form,

retaining a chorus, a restricted number of characters on stage, and other elements of Athenian tragedy, the conditions under which his plays were presented were quite different from those of Euripidean drama. Above all, it is generally surmised that they were not performed on stage, but read aloud,[3] with the consequence that they tend to be written as a series of set speeches whose effect depends on the rhetoric of the moment, rather than in the variety of styles enabling the greater realism employed by Euripides. This is often not to modern taste: even Seneca's translator complains of 'excess of rhetoric, irrelevance, iteration, banality, bathos'.[4] Moreover, his tragedy tends simply to oppose good and evil, without the moral shades of grey that are vital in Euripides.

Seneca sets his play in Athens, not Trozen, and the Chorus are Athenian citizens. A long prologue by Hippolytus opens it, as he urges his companions on to the hunt, and invokes Artemis – here, more the goddess of the hunt than of chastity. Phaedra then bemoans to her Nurse that she is banished from Crete to a hostile land (a theme not prominent in Euripides, but taken up by many successors) and that her cold husband is absent, capturing the queen of the underworld – another contrast with Euripides' devoted Theseus. Meanwhile she is wretched and longs to be out hunting. Like Euripides' Phaedra, she recalls her mother's unhappy love, but ascribes their misfortunes in love to a curse that Venus (the Greek Aphrodite) had imposed on all descendants of the Sun, because he had once revealed her adultery with Mars to her husband.[5] Venus herself does not appear in person in the play. The Nurse is not Euripides' amoral intellectual, but a conventional and prudent woman, who urges her to repress her love for the good of her family, and because Theseus will be cruel to her, as he was to the Amazon. When Phaedra eventually agrees to do so, however, and determines that suicide is her only remedy, the Nurse, with a startling lack of the psychological realism that pervaded Euripides' equivalent scene, volunteers instead to importune Hippolytus. After a long choral interlude hymning the power of love, a scene closely modelled on Euripides' *Hippolytus* follows, in which the Nurse and Phaedra wonder what to do about her sickness. Since her secret is already revealed, it lacks the suspense of Euripides' scene and is quite out of place.

Hippolytus then arrives, and in a long speech the Nurse extols the joys of love (520ff.) He replies, not with the anger and visceral disgust of Euripides' character, but in a speech full of Roman commonplaces on the moral superiority of the country to the city. Tacked onto it are rather perfunctory denunciations of female wickedness, and although when the Nurse presses him, he produces further hostilities, he is not nearly as violent as our Hippolytus. Just as the Nurse is giving up, Phaedra appears, and decides that she will try to persuade him after all. Hippolytus asks his 'mother' what is wrong. Phaedra replies that he should call her his servant instead, since she would do anything for him. As in Ovid, and perhaps the first *Hippolytus*, she even offers him the throne in Theseus' absence. Hippolytus is shocked but promises to look after his brothers and Phaedra until Theseus' return.

Phaedra interprets his innocent words to suit herself, and they converse at cross-purposes, rather as Euripides' Phaedra does with the Nurse, but finally she admits that she loves not Theseus, but Hippolytus himself. She flings herself at his feet, and he departs in shock, leaving his sword behind. The Nurse immediately makes a counter-charge of rape against him, using his abandoned sword to prove his guilt. Theseus then arrives, and, as in Euripides, he is disconcerted to hear lamentation. This time, however, it comes from a still-living Phaedra who, after some preamble, accuses Hippolytus of rape. At the end of a long speech which has some elements in common with its Euripidean equivalent, Theseus curses him with the last of Neptune's (Poseidon's) curses. The following messenger's

113

speech (1229ff.) is more graphic even than Euripides' in its descriptions of the bull and of Hippolytus' injuries.

After a lament from the Chorus, Phaedra comes to view the remains of her stepson. She is remorseful, and in a dramatic speech confesses all and kills herself. In a scene notorious even by the standards of Senecan drama, Theseus attempts to put the broken bits of Hippolytus' body back together (1541ff.): 'Here is a piece ... what part of you it is I cannot tell, but it is part of you (!)' The play ends with Theseus' orders for lamentation, and burial for the remains of Hippolytus and Phaedra.

In European literature, under Seneca's influence, the story of Hippolytus and Phaedra particularly attracted French writers. Although the Italians translate Seneca in 1488 and Euripides in 1504, Italy essentially ignores Phaedra until d'Annunzio's peculiar rendition of the story in 1909, and though Seneca's influence on English drama was great, this story is French territory as far back as Robert Garnier's *Hippolyte* (1573), which combines a Senecan plot with a Christian theology based on predestination: thus it opens with a monologue by Theseus' dead father Aegeus, which establishes immediately that the family is damned by a curse. Since, like Garnier's, most of the numerous French Hippolytus dramas are closer to Seneca, I will deal with them only briefly,[6] but some do have original touches which demand mention both to show how flexible and enduring this myth has been and because some moderns have reworked the story in similar ways.

Certain conventions fix a great gulf between Euripides and French drama. The dignity of tragedy dictates that no play must contain any person or thing associated with the lower classes, so that the slave Nurse of Euripides must be transformed into a more respectable lady of the court who acts as a confidante. Most important is the idea of *galanterie*, which mandates that plays must have a love intrigue – Euripides' Aphrodite would have approved! By the seventeenth century Hippolytus' chastity seemed awkward and unnatural, so that dramatists deviate radically from Euripides' conception by incorporating into the story a woman who is Hippolytus' mistress and thus Phaedra's rival. This innovation has been traced to Puget de la Serre's *Amours de Diane et Hypolite*,[7] in which Diana herself (Artemis) loves Hippolytus (chastely, of course) but the jealous Phaedra falsely accuses Hippolytus to Theseus, and when he runs away, he dies in an 'accident'. This version is unusual in having Poseidon play no role in Hippolytus' death. Generally, even plots which jettison the other gods retain this part of the divine role in the story.[8]

In the mid-seventeenth century unrequited Platonic love was in fashion in court, and Gabriel Gilbert's *Hypolite ou le Garçon Insensible* (1646) offers an interesting variant on the Hippolytus theme. Here, Hippolytus burns hopelessly and platonically for a woman, who is – Phaedra herself! But since this would be adulterous, Gilbert cunningly removes the criminal element by making Phaedra engaged rather than married to Theseus, but unhappy with the arrangement, since Theseus has already been married to her sister Ariadne and is suspected of other affairs. Thus an affair between Hippolytus and Phaedra is in theory more admirable than one between Phaedra and Theseus. Hippolytus' hatred of women, of course, is suppressed, while in Mathieu Bidar's *Hippolyte* (1675), Phaedra openly loves Hippolytus, but he loves Cyane. Hippolytus acts as a kind of marriage guidance counsellor to his stepmother, encouraging her to marry his father Theseus, who adores her, but she is dissatisfied with this prospective husband, so writes a letter – not to Theseus, but Cyane, telling her that Hippolytus no longer loves her. When this evil plan fails, she accuses Hippolytus of mooning after her and wanting to kill the king. Even plays in which the original story has been carefully reworked must all end the same way, even when the new plot would not naturally seem to lead to Hippolytus' destruction – somehow he must always be falsely accused and die, even if his fate does not follow logically from what has already happened in the play. Thus, in Bidar's play, when Theseus shows Hippolytus Phaedra's letter, he meekly agrees to leave the court, even though it is obvious even to Cyane that the letter is false, and even though Theseus is surprised that he makes no protest, so that the usual events can take place.

1677 saw the production of two rival Phaedra plays, and though on the first night, that of Racine lost in popularity to that of Jacques Pradon, posterity has judged differently. In a strongly moralising preface, Racine explains his conception of the story. The Nurse is blamed for the false accusation, and though Phaedra initially acquiesces in the plan in her agitation, she soon rejects it in favour of the truth, thus preserving her goodness. Indeed, Hippolytus is not even accused of rape but of merely contemplating it. Racine also claims that Euripides' Hippolytus is too virtuous, so he makes him 'sin' by loving Aricie, the last surviving relative of Theseus' enemies, the Pallantidae. Thus, as in earlier French versions of the play, Hippolytus has a mistress and Phaedra a rival. The gods are absent from the play, but both Euripides and Seneca influence Racine's treatment of the story.

The play begins as Hippolytus talks to his confidant Theramenes, and we learn that Theseus is absent, Phaedra, representative of a decadent and defiled Cretan family, is dying and Hippolytus is in love for the first time, with Aricie, though their love is forbidden. The next scene strongly recalls Euripides, as Phaedra vacillates between desire and shame in the presence of her Nurse, Oenone. Eventually she admits that she fell in love with Hippolytus on her wedding day and since then has unsuccessfully tried to repress her feelings. It is then announced that Theseus is dead, and it is unclear who will succeed him – Hippolytus, Phaedra's son or even Aricie. Oenone advises that Phaedra's son should be his successor, leaving her free to marry Hippolytus.

Meanwhile, Aricie, believing that Hippolytus will not recall her from banishment, is surprised when he comes to revoke it, and even more when he confesses that he loves her. However, in the next scene, Phaedra declares her love to Hippolytus via the claim that the dead Theseus lives on in his son. Hippolytus, appalled, departs, leaving his sword. (Both elements are Senecan.) Phaedra is distressed that her secret is out and blames Oenone for earlier advising her against suicide. In a frenzy, she commands her to find Hippolytus and offer him the Athenian throne as an inducement to win him to her.

Theseus is, of course, alive. Phaedra is horrified at the news, and longs for death. Oenone, however, suggests that she should make a counter-accusation against Hippolytus to save her honour, using the sword as evidence of his guilt, and Phaedra acquiesces. When Theseus appears before her, Phaedra says that she must depart at once. Theseus is baffled by this, and when Hippolytus also declares his intention to leave Athens, he is distressed at the loveless welcome that his family is offering him. At Oenone's false accusation, however, he becomes furious at his son's apparent hypocrisy. In a scene reminiscent of its Euripidean original, he violently denounces Hippolytus and summons Neptune's power to destroy him. As in Euripides, this is the first time he has invoked the god. Though more attractive than his Euripidean counterpart, Hippolytus is similarly unable to prove his innocence to his father. Some of his arguments for the defence derive from Euripides, but he uses his love for Aricie as the clinching factor in his innocence. Theseus is sceptical and exiles him. Phaedra begs Theseus to spare him until she learns that Hippolytus has confessed his love for Aricie, whereupon she feels betrayed, frightened and uncertain. Oenone can only encourage her to pursue her love (cf. E. *Hipp.*

445ff.), but Phaedra, furious at being embroiled in this mess, drives her away.

Aricie begs Hippolytus to get his father to revoke the exile, but, since he trusts that Phaedra will be divinely punished, he will not reveal her guilt himself. Instead, he begs Aricie to elope with him, but must hastily leave as Theseus approaches. Theseus warns Aricie of Hippolytus' alleged dalliance with Phaedra, but – like Euripides' Chorus – she can only hint that all is not what it seems: following Hippolytus' example of sparing Phaedra's reputation, she cannot be explicit. Theseus summons Oenone for an explanation, but she has drowned herself, and Phaedra is raving. Theseus demands to see his son and prays to Neptune to revoke the curse. It is too late: Theramenes performs the role of messenger. Eventually Phaedra confesses her guilt and poisons herself, and Theseus expiates his guilt by honouring his dead son and adopting Aricie as his daughter.

Pradon differs from Racine in having a Phaedra who is only engaged to Theseus, and an Aricie who is Phaedra's confidante, which obviously creates interesting dramatic possibilities: Hippolytus is exiled when Theseus finds him at Phaedra's feet and assumes the worst, when in fact he is trying to stop her harming his beloved Aricie. Edmund Smith's *Phaedra and Hippolytus* (1707) also owed much to Racine, although it was set in Crete where Hippolytus is in love with Ismena, a captive princess, and not the Nurse, but Lycon, a wicked politician, is responsible for Hippolytus' destruction.

Robert Browning's poem 'Artemis Prologises' dramatises the resurrection of Hippolytus first narrated by Virgil. He imagines the goddess standing over Hippolytus' corpse alongside Asclepius. She recounts his sad story and then Asclepius brings him back to life. She then bears him away so that he can worship her eternally. Swinburne's poem 'Phaedra' offers a more lurid account of her encounter with Hippolytus:

6. The Afterlife of Hippolytus

> Come take thy sword and slay;
> Let me not starve between desire and death
> But send me on my way with glad wet lips ...
> ... Yea, if mine own blood ran upon my mouth,
> I would drink that ...

Although the popularity of the translations of Ulrich von Wilamowitz-Moellendorf in Germany and Gilbert Murray in England ensured the staging of the *Hippolytus* in Austria, Germany and England in the early twentieth century, it has been performed on the modern stage less frequently than plays such as Sophocles' *Oedipus the King*, or Aeschylus' *Agamemnon*, whether because of the peculiarity of its main character, or because its subjects of passion and revenge are considered to have less tragic dignity than those of some other tragedies.[9] It has, however, been a rich source of inspiration for original or experimental versions of the story, which range from adaptations which simply modernise the play, to work whose inspiration is Euripidean but whose form is not classical.

Jules Dassin's film *Phaedra* (1962) belongs to the former category. His Theseus is a Greek shipping magnate called Thanos and Hippolytus is Alexis, a son by a previous marriage to an English woman.[10] The plot is Euripidean, but much modernised – the gods are absent and the 'chariot' that kills Alexis is an Aston Martin. As in a number of other modern versions, the relationship between Phaedra and 'Hippolytus' is fully consummated. Dassin makes the story a somewhat melodramatic conflict between erotic passion and family ties in high society.

David Rudkin's 'version' of the *Hippolytus* (1980) attempts to remove all the ancient elements that he presumes are incomprehensible for a modern audience, on the principle that 'we might only ever approach the "original experience" of Athenian tragedy by first expunging from it every element we think of as "Greek" '.[11] Thus – as for some critics cited in Chapter 5 – the gods become 'forces', while certain parts of the play, such as the prologue and Theseus' speech, have been altered and expanded with information thought necessary for a modern audience. The Chorus metamorphoses into 'a young woman'. Disappointingly, the wordplay that is so striking in Euripides has vanished, even though it is quite possible to reproduce much of it in English, and modernisation has sometimes produced a banal effect. Thus the old servant urges Hippolytus to heed not a proud goddess, but 'your sexuality', which seems trite by comparison. However, in spite of his determination to update the story, Rudkin proves unable to dispense with the bull from the sea. As he says, it 'defies all rationalisation', but after his excision of the rest of Euripides' 'Greekness' to aid modern comprehension, the retention of this one element is jarring, and his policy of 'de-Greeking' the *Hippolytus* actually makes it harder to understand in some places, not easier.

Another innovative but generally more successful adaptation is Kenneth Rexroth's *Phaedra*, which opens with anxious talk from the Chorus about their queen's sickness, Theseus' absence in the underworld and Hippolytus' indifference to city affairs. Their Hippolytus is a reformed debauchee who has been visiting the city but is now returning to his home in the woods. Then Phaedra is brought in, and in a scene of Euripidean inspiration, though not content, she raves and longs to return to Crete, before gathering her strength to dance a strange and alarming 'Minotaur dance': Rexroth emphasises the Cretan exoticism which is only embryonic in Euripides but already more noticeable in Seneca. Hippolytus now returns because he had left his sword behind – Phaedra had put it in her bed, to his disgust! – and in conversation with her, he reveals that in fact he does not hunt, because he has vowed never to take any life to atone for previous lust and violence: instead he serves an Artemis who is the goddess of peace and renunciation. Phaedra is amazed that he is not the cold rationalist Greek of her assumptions. She cries and Hippolytus asks her what is wrong: after some hesitation, he is her partner in a dance. A blackout follows.

Rexroth makes Euripides' chaste huntsman neither a huntsman nor chaste, since we now learn that he has loved Phaedra for ten years and Artemis has been merely a surrogate. In a speech influenced by Virgil's *Aeneid*, Phaedra urges that they escape to a place in Italy, settled by Trojan and Cretan fugitives, who will one day crush Theseus' heirs. She means, of course, Rome. Hippolytus answers that all he desires is her and they dance again, only to leap apart at Theseus' arrival. Phaedra runs out and Theseus recounts his adventures in Hades, which include sex with Persephone and escape home on the very bull once loved by Pasiphae, a 'sort of relative' that had been lost in the underworld years ago; it is now in the stable with his horses. In another surprise for those familiar with Euripides, Hippolytus confesses his feelings for Phaedra, and far from being angry, Theseus is delighted, both because it proves the resemblance between himself and his son, and because he and Phaedra are unhappily married. He even offers them Crete as a kingdom. As with some of the French versions of the myth, certain events have to happen even if they seem slightly illogical, and here, though no longer Euripides' sexless being, Hippolytus is still high-minded enough to be appalled at Theseus' casual attitude, and at his career of violence and lust, and storms out. Phaedra, having heard the conversation, kills herself with Hippolytus' sword: Hippolytus is killed by the bull which had escaped from the stables. Theseus laments the terrible discrepancy between his intentions and the 'disaster' they bring.[12]

Robinson Jeffers' *The Cretan Woman* (1954) is perhaps the most successful of these creative adaptations. His chief innovation in the character of Hippolytus is in making him explicitly homosexual. Aphrodite is a presence in the play, but Artemis is absent. The Chorus is reduced to three old female dependents of the queen who begin the play by coming to the palace to request food, but Phaedra's maid Selene denies their request since Phaedra is unwell. We then see the lovesick Phaedra, who is struggling to restrain her desire, though Selene warns her that her feelings are hopeless, since Hippolytus dislikes women. Phaedra announces her intention to die and returns to the palace. Now Aphrodite appears, and in a speech resembling Euripides' prologue, describes her power to harm and help. Making explicit what Euripides implies, she asserts that she has some pity for human beings, but divinities are a force of nature and neither mercy nor fear move them.

In the next scene, we meet Hippolytus and his friends. He and the slightly effeminate Alcyon are clearly lovers, and when his friend Andros commends women to him, he prefers to 'worship the great goddess of love at a great distance' (cf. *Hipp.* 113), and rejects deities that are worshipped at night (cf. *Hipp.* 106.) Selene then asks him to visit the dying Phaedra, and when he does so, Phaedra asks him why he is cold towards her. He is courteous but uncomprehending and eventually tactfully explains that he does not care for women – if he did, he might have loved her. Now she becomes more impassioned, comparing Greek savagery with the sophistication of the sensuous Cretans, and begging for Hippolytus' love until he can stand no more and departs.

A messenger brings news that Theseus is well but concerned about an oracle which says that his house is on fire. Phaedra cryptically comments that 'a worse burns' (cf. Euripides fr. 429), and an alarmed Selene swears the Chorus to secrecy on his return. Now, in a lyric duet with the Chorus, Phaedra expresses shame and anguish, though she resolves not to betray Theseus and, like Euripides' Phaedra, states her desire to be remembered as chaste. On Theseus' return, however, she hints, without saying his name (cf. *Hipp.* 352), that Hippolytus has raped her. Theseus vacillates between belief and scepticism, while Phae-

dra bitterly upbraids him for violent pseudo-heroism and regrets having married him. Eventually, he asks the truth from
Hippolytus and the two argue inconclusively. When Hippolytus
appeals to the Chorus, they offer no help since they are sworn
to secrecy. Theseus kills Hippolytus and also Alcyon, who had
tried to defend his lover, and Phaedra confesses the truth,
though she also addresses venomous words to Theseus before
hanging herself. Left with the corpse, Theseus unsuccessfully
offers all three of his prayers to Poseidon to resurrect Hippolytus. The play ends with the arrival, not of an absolving
Artemis, but a cold Aphrodite, 'not extremely sorry for the woes
of men'. For Jeffers more explicitly than for Euripides, perhaps
because his Hippolytus is more normal than Euripides', Hippolytus' fate warns the audience that they too are vulnerable:
'There is always a knife in the flowers. There is always a lion
just beyond the firelight.'

Manuel Fernandes' play *Hippolyta*[13] is set in a lower middle-
class American family. The gods are eliminated, and the sexes
of Euripides' tragedy are changed so that it becomes a topical
story of a stepdaughter sexually abused by a stepfather whose
guilt is not believed by her mother. This is an interesting
change, given modern critics' interest in Hippolytus' own femininity (cf. Chapter 5, pp. 94-5), and the modern world's greater
affinity with Phaedra than with Hippolytus. Just as the guilty
Phaedra accuses Hippolytus of rape to clear her own name, so
in this play, after a failed attempt at rape, the stepfather claims
before departing that Hippolyta had been making advances to
him. The mother 'exiles' Hippolyta by ordering her to leave the
house, but she shoots herself and her mother is left to ponder
what she comes to realise is her own mistake. By contrast,
Steven Porter's abridged and modernised *Hippolytus* makes
Hippolytus' fanaticism representative of conservative religious
fanaticism in the United States: its reviewer comments, 'It's no
coincidence that Hippolytus' violent diatribe about the inherent

wickedness of women sounds very similar to the preachings at a Southern Baptist ... convention.'[14]

Eugene O'Neill's *Desire Under the Elms* transports the plot of an incestuous relationship between a stepmother and stepson to a New England farm, where Phaedra becomes Abbie Putnam and Hippolytus, Eben Cabot. The result is a kind of Euripidean *Cold Comfort Farm*, in which the Hippolytus figure consummates the relationship with his stepmother in the parlour in which his birth mother had been laid out after her death. Abbie's feelings for Eben are an explicit and uncomfortable mixture of maternal and sexual. They even have a child together, which Abbie eventually murders as a proof of her love for Eben. O'Neill used the *Hippolytus* as a model, but his play has little in common with its original, and it is entirely comprehensible on its own terms without any reference to Euripides. Because of this, it is distinct from the plays previously discussed, which cannot be understood without some acknowledgement of their Euripidean original. O'Neill's play goes about as far as it can from Euripides while still being classifiable as a Hippolytus play. Some critics take the concept of 'Hippolytus plot' much further than this, however, and classify all plots in which an older married woman falls in love with a younger man or her stepson as Hippolytus stories.[15] Constraints of space forbid me to do the same.

O'Neill's theme is classical, but his setting is not. By contrast, D'Annunzio's *Fedra* (1909) combines two classical stories in which Theseus has a part – that of Phaedra's love for Hippolytus and the story of the seven against Thebes – in a play whose inspiration and setting are unimpeachably classical but which has little in common with Euripides in sensibility. A more complex case is the work of the poet 'H.D.' who reworks the story completely, yet manages to highlight certain elements that lurk in the background of Euripides. She was particularly interested in the Hippolytus myth, and her collected poems contain four monologues on the story.[16] In 'Hippolytus Temporizes' Hippolytus is uncertain about his chastity: each stanza begins with a declaration of loyalty to Artemis, ceding to a parenthetical outpouring of desire for Phaedra. 'Phaedra' expresses sympathy for the lovesick queen, while 'She Contrasts with Herself Hippolyta' and 'She Rebukes Hippolyta' are meditations on Hippolytus' mother. In her play also called *Hippolytus Temporizes*, H.D. uses the Hippolytus story to dramatise conflicts between spiritual and physical love. This Hippolytus resembles Euripides' in his disdain for the city and kingship, but he is in love with a rather grumpy Artemis. Even chaste devotion annoys this solitary and cold goddess who wants to be not just a goddess but a pure spirit. In fact, H.D.'s portrayal conveys much of the symbolism of Artemis that critics such as Dodds see in Euripides. H.D.'s Hippolytus feels explicit sexual desire towards Artemis: Euripides' does not, but he does characterise his relationship with her in vocabulary which has sexual connotations (cf. Chapter 4, p. 68 & n. 12, p. 134).

Phaedra is the representative of Aphrodite (who does not appear in person), and, like some other Phaedras, hates Theseus and a Greece lacking the sensuality of her native Crete. She tricks Hippolytus into sleeping with her by disguising herself as Artemis, and the morning after, the two confront each other angrily. Hippolytus believes that he has consummated his love with Artemis, and will not believe those, including Phaedra, who tell him otherwise. Indeed, he rebukes her so violently for daring to venture into Artemis' territory that she becomes distraught and hangs herself. Hippolytus himself rides off in triumph. When Artemis discovers what has happened, she is furious and prophesies his death, which duly comes to pass. The final act concerns the question of Hippolytus' resurrection in a dialogue between Artemis and the healing god Helios/Paian, who wishes to restore him, but ultimately he is consigned to death. Here, Hippolytus represents not chastity but erotic ambition, proved by his vulnerability to Phaedra's trick, while Artemis desires an unfeasible mixture of cold independence and worship by others. The style of the play is highly original. John Walsh notes H.D.'s hypnotic repetition and 'trancelike stammering induced by an overwhelming experience',[17] and compares her style to that of modernist composers such as Stravinsky and Orff.

Three modern novels set the Hippolytus story in the broader context of the Theseus myth. André Gide's *Thésée* purports to be the autobiography of the aged Theseus who had intended to tell his life story to Hippolytus. Since, to his sorrow, his son is dead, Theseus can now include some of his love affairs in his story, since Hippolytus was 'amazingly prudish' and he never 'dared' mention them in front of him. Gide's Theseus met Phaedra on Crete on his mission to kill the Minotaur.[18] Though it was her elder sister Ariadne who eloped with him, Theseus found her clinging and annoying, and much preferred Phaedra. Thus, by disguising her as her young brother, he took her from Crete and back to Athens. On his return, he was faithful to her, but the gods punished him for his conceit at his success. He had taken her at such a young age that he did not realise that she had a genetic propensity for perverse love, or that she had previously offended Aphrodite. The age gap between them was also too great. Meanwhile Hippolytus grew up to love hunting and hate women, and Phaedra fell in love with him. Like Rexroth's, this is a forgiving Theseus – he understands the attraction she felt and simply regrets believing her accusation. Now he is old and alone, but still glorious, and though he has no family, the creation of Athens is his comfort.

In Mary Renault's *The King Must Die*, the young Theseus had killed the Minotaur and taken control of Crete, where he first met the child Phaedra. *The Bull from the Sea* is its sequel. Like Gide's, Renault's Theseus is the story's narrator and events are seen from his perspective. His great love is Hippolytus' mother, who is killed when her fellow Amazons invade Attica. He marries Phaedra for political reasons, to retain control of Crete, and although he does not find her unattractive, this decadent Cretan from 'rotten stock' (p. 38) is not his soul-mate. As in June Brindel's novel, the patriarchal religion of Theseus and the older female-centred goddess-religion are in conflict. Renault portrays Theseus' religion more favourably than the sinister and primitive goddess religion.

Hippolytus will be a better king than Akamas, his half-brother by Phaedra, as Theseus realises, but he is, of course, committed to his mother's virgin goddess-worship, and rejects sex and kingship. This Hippolytus, however, lacks the cold priggishness of which Euripides' Hippolytus is accused, and Theseus is more sympathetic to him. As Artemis' servant, he loves animals and is a gifted healer. When Phaedra visits Theseus in Athens, Hippolytus cures her of a headache and she sends for him regularly, until he seems uncomfortable and insists on escaping to Trozen. After a time, Phaedra persuades Theseus to go there: she is unwell and nobody (except readers familiar with Euripides) knows why. The visit is difficult: Hippolytus is moody and Phaedra's health remains bad. As they are about to return to Athens, Theseus hears Phaedra cry 'Rape!' and sees Hippolytus fleeing. When questioned, she claims that Hippolytus had promised the Goddess that by marrying Phaedra he could re-establish goddess-worship in Greece. Theseus believes her and curses Hippolytus. Hippolytus says nothing and departs, but when Akamas warns Theseus that Phaedra was lying, Theseus runs to find him. Hippolytus accepts death magnanimously and forgives his father. Theseus is furious at Phaedra's calculated lies: 'Many a night she must have lain with these words in mind, trying them this way and that' (p. 215). His words recall those of Euripides' Phaedra about her moral cogitations in the long nights (*Hipp.* 373ff.) but contrast with them. In a horrific climax unique among the stories discussed here,

Theseus actually strangles her and then fakes a suicide note admitting that she slandered Hippolytus. We are apparently not meant to condemn him for doing so. Overall, Renault is more generous to Theseus and Hippolytus at Phaedra's expense than Euripides or anyone else.

June Brindel's *Phaedra: a Novel of Ancient Athens* (1985) covers similar ground, but is explicitly anti-patriarchal. As in Gide, Phaedra is a young girl when she is carried off from Crete by Theseus, and the story is narrated by the older girl who had looked after her since then. Phaedra is the last representative of the old goddess-religion, and the struggle between the supporters of the new and old religions dominates this book even more than Renault's. Because of her ties to the mother goddess, Phaedra is important for Theseus as a means of keeping his power over the Aegean, so he marries her. Brindel suggests that Phaedra is an actual incarnation of the mother-goddess, and Hippolytus, the male consort that accompanies the female in Cretan art (pp. 140, 224): hence she hints that Hippolytus and Phaedra have a special relationship as he grows older, although it is not the simple sexual relationship of the usual story. Brindel's feminist slant makes her version of the story very different from that of Euripides, but even so, the usual things happen: Theseus kills Hippolytus and Phaedra dies, though Poseidon is absent, and there is no false accusation. In an interesting coda, the narrator explains the worship of Athena in the patriarchal religion as an adaptation of the old goddess-worship, and also claims that she has told the truth about Phaedra and Hippolytus, but the standard (misogynistic) story of Phaedra's seduction of Hippolytus was invented by the court bards and became the normal form of the story.[19] She also mentions Hippolytus' resurrection and translation to Aricia as a servant of the Mother Goddess, of whom Artemis is one manifestation.

The Phaedra and Hippolytus myth has also attracted composers. Rameau's *Hippolyte et Aricie* (1733) focuses on the eponymous young lovers, and Hippolytus is ultimately restored to life happily ever after. Music by Gluck (*Fedra*, 1744), Massenet (overture for *Phèdre*, 1873) and Honegger (music for d'Annunzio's *Fedra*, 1926) has been also inspired by the story, as was Cocteau's ballet *Phèdre* in 1950. One of Britten's last works (1975) was a solo cantata entitled 'Phaedra' whose text was from Robert Lowell's translation of Racine. On 26 August 1995, George Roumanis' opera *Ode to Phaedra* was performed by Opera San Jose, in California. According to its press release, this is a lyric opera in which the story is viewed from Phaedra's side. As Euripides prophesied, more truly than he was aware, 'Phaedra's love for Hippolytus will not fall away in silence.'

Notes

1. Euripides and His World

1. Stevens, 'Euripides', pp. 87-90. For works whose full title is not given in these notes, see the guide to further reading at the end of the book, where the short title is keyed to a full title.

2. Stevens, 'Euripides', pp. 92-3.

3. The topic has given rise to a huge amount of literature. The works that have given me the greatest help in writing this section are Blundell, *Women*; Just, *Women*, Gould, 'Law, Custom and Myth' and D. Cohen, 'Seclusion, Separation and the Status of Women', *Greece and Rome* 36 (1989), pp. 3-15.

4. Pandora: Hesiod, *Theogony* 585-612; *Works and Days* 90-105. Women as a drain on men: *Works and Days* 373-5, 702-5, cf. 519-21.

5. Just, *Women*, pp. 161-93.

6. Blundell, *Women*, p. 72ff.

7. A sentiment from the funeral oration attributed to Pericles by Thucydides, 2.45.2

8. Cf. J. Henderson, 'Women and the Athenian Dramatic Festivals', *Transactions of the American Philological Society* 121 (1991), pp. 133-47. A serious challenge to his conclusions is, however, offered by Simon Goldhill, 'Representing Democracy: Women at the Great Dionysia' in *Ritual, Finance, Politics: Democratic Accounts Presented to David Lewis* (Oxford: Clarendon Press, 1994), pp. 347-69.

9. Especially Just, *Women*, pp. 106-21 and Cohen (cited in n. 3).

10. G. Kerferd, *The Sophistic Movement* (Cambridge: Cambridge University Press, 1981) and Guthrie, *The Sophists* are particularly helpful accounts of sophistic thought.

2. Tragedy and the Hippolytus Story

1. A kind of burlesque of some of the myths of the preceding tragedies, performed by actors wearing tragic dress and a chorus

131

dressed as satyrs. Aristotle suggests that tragedy actually developed from satyr play.

2. On all matters to do with *chorêgoi*, see now Peter Wilson, *The Athenian Institution of the Khoregia: the Chorus, the City and the Stage* (Cambridge: Cambridge University Press, 2000).

3. The bibliography on the ancient theatre is huge. Pickard-Cambridge, *Dramatic Festivals*, remains fundamental. Other helpful treatments include Taplin, *Greek Tragedy*, Gould, 'Tragedy in Performance', R. Rehm, *Greek Tragic Theatre* (London: Routledge, 1992), J. Michael Walton, *Greek Theatre Practice* (Connecticut: Greenwood Press, 1980), while Easterling, *Cambridge Companion*, pp. 3-90, contains several very helpful essays.

4. Isocrates, *On the Peace*, 82. See Goldhill, 'The Great Dionysia', pp. 99-106, and now Goldhill's amplification of his position in 'Civic Ideology and the Problem of Difference: the Politics of Aeschylean Tragedy, Once Again', *Journal of Hellenic Studies* 120 (2000), pp. 34-56, esp. 34-47.

5. A twelve-syllable line, divided into three groups of four, of which the first syllable can be long or short, with the remaining three syllables in the order long-short-long. Thus: x–u–| x–u–| x–u–. Variants are also possible.

6. Aristotle, *Poetics* ch. 13, p. 44 in *The Poetics of Aristotle*, translated by Stephen Halliwell (London: Duckworth, 1987).

7. But, for a healthy dose of scepticism, see J. Gibert, 'Euripides' Hippolytus Plays – Which Came First?', *Classical Quarterly* 47 (1997), pp. 85-97.

8. The numbering is from the edition of the tragic fragments by August Nauck, *Tragicorum Graecorum Fragmenta*, 2nd edn. (Hildesheim: Olms, 1964). Halleran, *Commentary*, pp. 25-37, provides an excellent translation and commentary on the fragments and their relationship to the first play.

9. See Barrett, *Commentary*, p. 18; Roisman, *Nothing is What It Seems*, pp. 12-15.

10. A fragmentary papyrus which seems to recount the plot of the first *Hippolytus* may make reference to Trozen, and W. Luppe, 'Die Hypothesis zum Ersten "Hippolytos" ', *Zeitschrift für Papyrologie und Epigraphik* 102 (1994), pp. 23-39, takes it as proof that the first play was also set in Trozen. However, the fragmentary state of the papyrus makes this less than certain.

3. A Summary of the Play

1. A town near Athens, famous for a cult of Demeter and Persephone that was open to all free Greeks and promised a happy existence in the afterlife to all initiates.

2. His cousins, but this does not necessarily reflect badly on him, since mythology always portrays them as destructive: the purification is a ritual requirement.

3. *Aidôs* is defined by W.S. Barrett (*Commentary*, pp. 171-2) as 'reverence' or 'the feeling of "not quite liking" which inhibits ... natural ... self-seeking in the face of the requirements of morality.' It can include the English 'shame' or 'self-restraint', but no English word covers all its range of meanings. It is a vitally important word in the *Hippolytus*: see Chapters 4 and 5.

4. The words 'arrogant' and 'proud' are a pun in Greek which will be discussed in Chapter 4.

5. Also called Britomartis, and a goddess of the wild identified with Artemis.

6. On supplication, see J. Gould, 'Hiketeia', *Journal of Hellenic Studies* 93 (1973), pp. 74-103. Supplication was a kind of ritual abasement, in which an inferior touched the face or knees of a superior and asked for protection or some other boon. Generally speaking, accepting a supplication is a moral imperative.

7. Metre emphasises content here, as she moves from emotionally distraught lyric metre to a calm, logical speech in iambic trimeter.

4. The Major Themes of the Play

1. Cf. p. 32 above. The Chorus' suggestions contain other ironies as well, especially their speculation that she has somehow offended Artemis (141ff.).

2. The association in Greek thought of riding with sex is well-documented and ancient.

3. M. Orban, '*Hippolyte*: Palinodie ou revanche?' *Les Etudes Classiques* 49 (1981), pp. 3-17 connects Phaedra's ambiguity here with her heritage as Pasiphae's daughter. As the Minotaur's half-sister, her impulse is to conceal; as the Sun god's granddaughter, her instinct is to reveal.

4. This is not the only possible translation, as will be seen in the next chapter, but it is the one which I think makes best sense of the Greek.

5. For the dispute on whether or not *aidôs* itself is actually pleasurable, or simply something like pleasure that hinders right action, see Chapter 5, p. 98.

6. *Orthoepeia* – finding accurate terminology for things – is a particular interest of some sophists of the day.

7. Less explicit examples of concern for appearance are found at 420, where she hopes that she 'may never be caught' shaming Theseus, and at 430 that she may never 'be seen' among adulterous females. While in itself, 'may I not be seen to' could simply amount to 'may I not', in the context of 403-4, which is so explicit about concealment of bad conduct, these lines acquire a more problematic aspect.

8. 'I will arrange my own affairs *well*' (709); 'I have a plan to provide an *honourable* life for my children' (717); 'Never will I *shame* my Cretan house' (719); 'Another sharing in my trouble will learn *to be virtuous*' (731).

9. The divinely-loved mortals whom she mentions are inauspicious role models (like those cited by the Chorus at 545 and 555f.), since the gods' love causes them both to come to sad ends.

10. *Commentary on Euripides' Bacchae* (Oxford: Clarendon Press, 1960), p. xlvi.

11. Agriculture and sexuality are commonly associated in the ancient world: '*sperma*' literally means 'seed', and sexual metaphors of ploughing are found, e.g. in Sophocles *Antigone* 569. Scholars note that meadows are often sites of erotic activity (e.g. *Homeric Hymn to Demeter* 1-29 and Sappho fr. 2) and thus that Hippolytus is trying to transform the meadow associated with Aphrodite into Artemis' place.

12. Commentators note that the verb *suneinai* used here and at 17, is often in a sexual context (as is the word *homilia*, ll.13, 1441), and that 17's phrase *suneinai parthenôi* ('have intercourse with the virgin') is paradoxical and draws attention to Hippolytus' unnatural life.

13. W.D. Smith, 'Staging in the Central Scene of the *Hippolytus*', *Transactions of the American Philological Association* 91 (1960), pp. 162-77 argues that since Phaedra apparently ignores Hippolytus' intent to keep his oath, she cannot have heard it, and must therefore be absent from the stage from 601-80. His arguments, though worth reading, are not conclusive and the usual assumption that Phaedra remains on stage, ignored by the raging Hippolytus (who does imply at 907 that he was aware of her presence) makes a far more powerful scene.

14. '*Semnon*', in yet another play on the quality that Hippolytus shares with Aphrodite but destroys him.

15. A similarly practical meaning of 'hypocritically high-minded' is assigned to *semnon* by both the Nurse (characterising Phaedra's attempts at honourably suppressing her love, 490-1) and by Theseus (characterising Hippolytus' protestations of innocence, 957ff., 1064). This meaning contrasts sharply with the moral connotations ascribed to it by Hippolytus.

16. The interest in sophistic teaching in Athens at the time makes this a question of particular relevance.

17. *Dissas*, the same word used for Phaedra's two kinds of shame at 387.

18. He calls him an Orphic (a believer in asceticism to purify the soul, vegetarianism and perhaps sexual restraint), using the term not literally, but to denote a puritan suspected of hypocrisy or charlatanism.

19. The messenger's speech is particularly full of symbolism. The bull recalls Phaedra's inheritance from her mother Pasiphae and is a metaphor both for an irrepressible sexuality, and more generally for the wild forces in the world that transcend human control, which were particularly fascinating to Euripides. The imagery of the swelling and gushing wave (1210f.) is clearly sexual, and commentators have written perceptively on the connections of Aphrodite with the sea in the play. Freud in *The Id and the Ego* (*Collected Works*, vol. 19, p. 25) compared the Id to a pair of runaway horses.

20. The word is used of Hippolytus' relationship with Artemis at l. 19, but also of Theseus' marriage to Phaedra, l. 838, which is the companionship appropriate and desirable for human beings.

21. This conception is at least as old as Homer: compare *Odyssey* 6.328-9 and 13.341-3.

22. *Hipp*. 120. A similar plea to a god is made at Euripides *Bacchae* 1348.

23. An excellent discussion of this kind of conception of the gods in the context of broader questions of Athenian religious belief is found in R. Parker, 'Gods Cruel and Kind: Tragic and Civic Theology', in C. Pelling, *Greek Tragedy and the Historian* (Oxford: Clarendon Press, 1997), pp. 143-61.

24. Halleran, *Commentary*, pp. 243-5 summarises the arguments very effectively. See also Barrett, 366ff., and G.W. Bond, 'A Chorus in Hippolytus: Manuscript Text versus Dramatic Realism', *Hermathena* 129 (1980), pp. 59-63.

25. And as is common in sophistically-influenced rhetoric, in which argument '*kata to eikos*' ('according to probability') is frequently employed.

5. Critical Views of Euripides and Hippolytus

1. Michelini, *Euripides*, pp. 3-51.

2. Gilbert Murray, *Euripides and His Age* (Oxford: Oxford University Press, 1946).

3. A.W. Verrall, *Euripides, the Rationalist: A Study in the History of Arts and Religion* (Cambridge: Cambridge University Press, 1895); E.R. Dodds, 'Euripides the Irrationalist', pp. 78-91 in *The Ancient Concept of Progress and other Essays in Greek Literature and Belief* (Oxford: Clarendon Press, 1973).

4. Philip Vellacott, *Ironic Drama: A Study of Euripides' Method and Meaning* (London & New York: Cambridge University Press, 1975), pp. 2-22.

5. Kovacs, *Heroic Muse*, pp. ix-x, and more generally, pp. 1-21.

6. Michelini, *Euripides*, pp. 277-80.

7. Barrett, *Commentary*, pp. 1-10; Louis Séchan, 'La Légende d'Hippolyte dans l'Antiquité', *Revue des Etudes Grecques* 40 (1911), pp. 105-51; H. Herter, 'Theseus und Hippolytos', *Rheinisches Museum für Philologie* 90 (1940), pp. 273-92; H.E. Barnes, *The Hippolytus of Drama and Myth* (Lincoln, NE: University of Nebraska Press, 1960, pp. 103-23.

8. B. Snell, *Scenes from Greek Drama* (Berkeley: University of California Press, 1964), pp. 23-46; C. Zintzen, *Analytisches Hypomnema zu Senecas Phaedra* (Meisenheim am Glan: Hain, 1960); O. Zwierlein, *Senecas Phaedra und Ihre Vorbilder* (Stuttgart: Steiner, 1987).

9. Barrett, *Commentary*, pp. 15-45; Halleran, *Commentary*, pp. 21-37.

10. E.M. Blaiklock, *The Male Characters of Euripides: a Study in Realism* (Wellington: New Zealand University Press, 1952).

11. Ernst Howald, *Die Griechische Tragödie* (Munich: Oldenbourg, 1930); Walter Zürcher, *Die Darstellung des Menschen im Drama des Euripides* (Basel: Reinhardt, 1947). A milder scepticism is found in John Gould, 'Dramatic Character and "Human Intelligibility" in Greek Tragedy', *Proceedings of the Cambridge Philological Society* 33 (1978), pp. 43-67.

12. Knox, *'Hippolytus'*, p. 205.

13. G. Devereux, *The Character of the Euripidean Hippolytos: an Ethno-Psychoanalytical Study* (Chico, CA: Scholars Press, 1985), p. 7.

14. A.J. Festugière, *Personal Religion Among the Greeks* (Berkeley: University of California Press, 1954), p. 11.

15. Grube, *Drama*, pp. 18-19.

16. Kovacs, *Heroic Muse*, pp. 23-9. For a vivid account of Greek attitudes to the pleasures of the flesh, see J. Davidson, *Courtesans and Fishcakes* (London: HarperCollins, 1997), especially pp. 139-82.

17. Kovacs, *Heroic Muse*, pp. 29-31; also Dimock, 'Virtue Rewarded', p. 241.

18. Festugière (cited in n. 14), pp. 13-14; André Rivier, *Essai sur le tragique d'Euripide*, 2nd ed. (Paris: Diffusion De Boccard, 1975), pp. 53-63; Dimock, 'Virtue Rewarded', p. 247.

19. W.B. Stanford, 'The Hippolytus of Euripides', *Hermathena* 63 (1944), pp. 11-17; Kovacs, *Heroic Muse*, p. 27.

20. Winnington-Ingram, 'Hippolytus', p. 176; Dimock, 'Virtue Rewarded', p. 245.

21. Roisman, *Nothing is What it Seems*, p. 141; Strauss, *Fathers and Sons*, p. 168.

22. Strauss, *Fathers and Sons*, p. 167; Grube, *Drama*, pp. 184-5; G.J. Fitzgerald, 'Misconception', p. 33; Roisman, *Nothing is What it Seems*, index, under 'bastardy'.

23. A. Rankin, 'Euripides' Hippolytus: A psychopathological hero', *Arethusa* 7 (1974), pp. 71-94; Devereux (cited in n. 13); Segal, 'Pentheus and Hippolytus on the Couch', pp. 268-82 discusses the methodology with sympathy and good sense.

24. Gould (cited in n. 11). See also Hugh Lloyd-Jones, 'Psychology and the Study of the Ancient World', pp. 152-89 in *Freud and the Humanities*, ed. Peregrine Horden (London/New York: Duckworth/St Martin's Press, 1985).

25. Roisman, *Nothing is What it Seems*, pp. 7-8, 29ff.; for her interpretation of Phaedra, see pp. 50-1.

26. Similarly E.M. Craik, 'Language of Sexuality and Sexual Inversion in Euripides' Hippolytus', *Acta Classica* 41 (1998), 29-44, esp. 34. For the homosexual Hippolytus, see also Chapter 6.

27. Segal, 'Pentheus and Hippolytus', pp. 274-82; Goldhill, *Reading Greek Tragedy*, pp. 107-37.

28. Devereux (cited in n. 13), pp. 19-23; Roisman, *Nothing is What it Seems*, pp. 27-30; Zeitlin, 'Power of Aphrodite', p. 66ff.

29. Zeitlin 'Power of Aphrodite', pp. 56-74.

30. Robin Mitchell-Boyask, 'Euripides' Hippolytus and the Trials of Manhood' in *Rites of Passage in Ancient Greece: Literature, Religion, Society*, ed. Mark Padilla (London: Associated University Presses, 1999), pp. 42-66.

31. Roisman, *Nothing is What it Seems*, pp. 47-107; Fitzgerald, 'Misconception', pp. 23-6.

32. Winnington Ingram, 'Hippolytus', pp. 179-81; Dodds, *'Aidôs'*, p. 103.

33. Knox, 'Hippolytus', p. 212; Winnington Ingram, 'Hippolytus', p. 180; Fitzgerald, 'Misconception', p. 25.

34. Snell (cited in n. 8), pp. 60-8; Dodds, *'Aidôs'*, p. 103; T.H. Irwin, 'Euripides and Socrates', *Classical Philology* 78 (1983), pp. 183-97.

35. Barrett, *Commentary*, p. 229.

36. Willink, 'Some Problems', p. 11ff., denies even that she means right conduct, but interprets the Greek to mean 'success in life' without moral implications.

37. For the former, Luschnig, *Time Holds the Mirror*, p. 42; for the latter, David Claus, 'Phaedra and the Socratic Paradox', *Yale Classical Studies* 22 (1972), p. 230; Kovacs, 'Shame, Honor, Pleasure', p. 291, Winnington-Ingram, 'Hippolytus', p. 178.

38. Bernd Manuwald, 'Phaidras Tragischer Irrtum', *Rheinisches Museum für Philologie* 122 (1979), pp. 134-8 (136-7); Barrett, *Commentary*, p. 229.

39. Willink, 'Some Problems', p. 14f., followed by Claus (cited in n. 37), p. 228 and Kovacs, 'Shame, Honor, Pleasure', pp. 293-4.

40. Willink, 'Some Problems', p. 15, Kovacs, 'Shame, Honor, Pleasure', p. 288.

41. Barrett, *Commentary*, p. 230.

42. Willink, 'Some Problems', p. 12; Claus (cited in n. 37), p. 228; Kovacs, 'Shame, Honor, Pleasure', p. 294.

43. Barrett, *Commentary*, p. 230; W.D. Furley, 'Phaidra's Pleasurable *Aidôs* (Eur. *Hipp.* 380-7)', *Classical Quarterly* n.s. 46 no. 1 (1996), pp. 84-90; Cairns, *Aidôs*, pp. 322-40; Bernard Williams, *Shame and Necessity* (Berkeley: University of California Press, 1993), pp. 225-30.

44. Barrett, *Commentary*, p. 230; Furley (cited in n. 43), p. 85f.

45. Hence Barrett suggests that the bad *aidôs* has prevented Phaedra from fighting her love and from killing herself, but this would hardly be pleasurable, and her failure to fight her love is hardly due to an emotion inhibiting wrongdoing. Cf. Kovacs, 'Shame, Pleasure and Honor', pp. 288-90.

46. Barrett, *Commentary*, p. 231, Dimock, 'Virtue Rewarded', p. 251; Furley (cited in n. 43), p. 88f.

47. Dodds, '*Aidôs*', p. 103; Charles Segal, 'Shame and Purity in Euripides' *Hippolytus*', *Hermes* 98 (1970), pp. 278-99 (284-5).

48. S. Kawashima, 'AIDOS and EYKLEIA: Another Interpretation of Phaedra's Long Speech in the *Hippolytus*', *Studi Italiani di Filologia e Cultura* 4 (1988), pp. 183-94.

49. Cairns, *Aidôs*, pp. 327-8; cf. Winnington Ingram, 'Hippolytus', pp. 174-7.

50. Craik (cited in n. 26); also '*Aidôs* in Euripides' *Hippolytos* 373-430: Review and Reinterpretation', *Journal of Hellenic Studies* 113 (1993), pp. 45-59. Conacher, *Euripidean Drama*, pp. 54-5 tends in the same direction. Against this position, see Furley (cited in n. 43), p. 85, Cairns, *Aidôs*, p. 322.

51. A.H. Sommerstein, 'Notes on Euripides' *Hippolytus*', *Bulletin of the Institute of Classical Studies* 35 (1988), pp. 23-41 (28); Kovacs, 'Shame, Pleasure, Honor', pp. 298-300.

52. Barnes (cited in n. 7), pp. 81-2; J. Gregory, *Euripides and the Instruction of the Athenians* (Ann Arbor: University of Michigan Press, 1991), pp. 51-84.

53. Knox, 'Hippolytus', p. 216; Zeitlin, 'Power of Aphrodite', p. 74ff.

54. Bernard Frischer, 'Concordia Discors and Characterisation in Euripides' Hippolytus', *Greek, Roman and Byzantine Studies* 11 (1970), pp. 85-100.

55. A. Lesky, *Greek Tragedy*, trans. Frankfurt (London & New York: Benn, 1965), p. 150.

56. Barnes (cited in n. 7), p. 78f.

57. Lattimore, 'Euripides' Phaedra' in Sanderson and Gopnik, pp. 283-96.

58. Barnes (cited in n. 7), pp. 82-3.

59. Lattimore, 'Euripides' Phaedra', pp. 291-2; K.J. Reckford, 'Phaedra and Pasiphae: The Pull Backward', *Transactions of the American Philological Society* 104 (1973), pp. 307-28.

60. Verrall (cited in n. 3); L.H.G. Greenwood, *Aspects of Euripidean Tragedy* (New York: Russell & Russell, 1953). Dimock, 'Virtue Rewarded', p. 240, also speaks of divine injustice.

61. Winnington-Ingram, 'Hippolytus', p. 188; Vellacott (cited in n. 4), pp. 19-22; Fitzgerald, 'Misconception', pp. 20, 29f., 34f.; J. Blomqvist 'Human and Divine Action in Euripides' *Hippolytus*', *Hermes* 110 (1982), pp. 398-414 (410-11); Barnes (cited in n. 7), p. 74.

62. Conacher, *Euripidean Drama*, pp. 28, 43f.

63. Dodds, 'Euripides the Irrationalist' (cited in n. 3), pp. 86-7.

64. Kovacs, *Heroic Muse*, p. 32.

65. To give one example, at *Iliad* 4.30ff., Hera's hatred of the Trojans inspires her to make a deal with Zeus whereby, if he allows Troy to be destroyed he can destroy any of the cities that are particularly dear to her. More generally on the topic, see M. Lefkowitz, ' "Impiety" and "Atheism" in Euripides' Dramas', *Classical Quarterly* 39 (1989), pp. 70-82, esp. 78. Conacher, *Euripidean Drama*, pp. 28-9, takes a very different line.

66. Malcolm Heath, *The Poetics of Greek Tragedy* (London: Duckworth, 1987), pp. 52-4.

67. Kovacs, *Heroic Muse*, p. 74.

68. Barnes (cited in n. 7), p. 72.

69. Gregory (cited in n. 52), pp. 52-5, 61-4, 74-9; Strauss, *Fathers and Sons*, pp. 166-75.

70. More specific allegory has also been suggested: for Strauss, *Fathers and Sons*, pp. 166-75, Hippolytus is an Alcibiades-figure; for Michelini, *Euripides*, pp. 304-10, he resembles Socrates.

71. H.C. Avery, 'My Tongue Swore But My Mind is Unsworn', *Transactions of the American Philological Society* 99 (1968), pp. 19-35; Luschnig, *Time Holds the Mirror*; Barbara E. Goff, *The Noose of Words: Readings of Desire, Violence, and Language in Euripides' Hippolytos* (Cambridge & New York: Cambridge University Press, 1990); C. Segal, *Euripides and the Poetics of Sorrow: Art, Gender, and Commemoration in Alcestis, Hippolytus, and Hecuba* (Durham, NC: Duke University Press, 1993), pp. 89-104, 136-9; Gary S. Meltzer, 'The "Just Voice" as Paradigmatic Metaphor in Euripides' Hippolytus', *Helios* 23.2 (1996), pp. 173-90.

72. See, for example, Knox, '*Hippolytus*', pp. 224-6; Charles Segal, 'The Tragedy of the Hippolytus: the Waters of Ocean and the Untouched Meadow', *Harvard Studies in Classical Philology* 70 (1965), pp. 117-69, reprinted in *Interpreting Greek Tragedy: Myth, Poetry, Text*, (Ithaca, NY: Cornell University Press, 1986), 165-221; Frischer (cited in n. 54); Shirley A. Barlow, *The Imagery of Euripides: a Study in the Dramatic Use of Pictorial Language* (London: Methuen, 1971); K.J.

Reckford, 'Phaedra, Hippolytus, Aphrodite', *Transactions of the American Philological Society* 103 (1972), pp. 405-32 (419-21); Zeitlin, 'Power of Eros', pp. 58-64; Goff (cited in n. 71); E.M. Craik (cited in n. 26).

73. Murray (cited in n. 2), pp. 18-19; Lucas, *Euripides and his Influence*, p. 36.

74. A helpful treatment of Euripides and women is given by N. Rabinowitz, *Anxiety Veiled: Euripides and the Traffic in Women* (Ithaca, NY: Cornell University Press, 1993), pp. 1-27.

6. The Afterlife of Hippolytus

1. Works that have proved particularly helpful to me in this chapter are the introduction to *Seneca's Phaedra*, ed. M. Coffey and R. Mayer (Cambridge: Cambridge University Press, 1990); Lucas, *Euripides and His Influence*; Francis, *Métamorphoses*.

2. For the Hippolytus myth in ancient art, see the *Lexicon Iconographicum Mythologiae Classicae* (Zurich: Artemis, 1981-1999), 5.1, pp. 445-64, under 'Hippolytus'.

3. In particular, textual inconsistencies suggest that Seneca's main concern was not stage action: for example, *Phaedra* 1156-8 and 1198 imply that Hippolytus' corpse is already on stage, but it is not actually brought in until 1244-74. On Seneca and performance, see the introduction to Coffey and Mayer (cited in n. 1).

4. E.F. Watling, *Seneca: Four Tragedies and Octavia* (Harmondsworth: Penguin, 1966), p. 25.

5. Seneca *Phaedra* 147ff. The story is first told in Homer, *Odyssey* 8.266-320.

6. For a full account of the tradition, see Francis, *Métamorphoses*.

7. Francis, *Métamorphoses*, p. 38ff.

8. Francis, *Métamorphoses*, pp. 41-2. Interestingly, a couple of modern adaptations retain Aphrodite, but remove Artemis, perhaps because she is less easy to make symbolic than Aphrodite.

9. *Hippolytos*, Ulrich von Wilamowitz-Moellendorf (Berlin: Weidmann, 1891); Gilbert Murray, *Euripides, translated into English rhyming verse* (London: G. Allen, 1908); H. Flashar, *Inszenierung der Antike: Das Griechische Drama auf der Buhne der Neuzeit 1585-1990* (Munich: Beck, 1991), pp. 123, 136. The figures quoted by J. Michael Walton, *Living Greek Theatre* (Westport, CT: Greenwood Press, 1987), pp. 288-9, are revealing: between 1954 and 1986, at Epidaurus in Greece, *Hippolytus* was performed three times as compared with ten for *Oedipus the King*, and Walton's statistics for other places where Greek tragedy is regularly performed are comparable. For details of American productions, see also Karelisa Hartigan, *Greek Tragedy on the American Stage: Ancient Drama in the Commercial Theatre 1882-*

1994 (Westport, CT: Greenwood Press, 1995), pp. 59-62, and of European productions, Flashar, p. 399.

10. The film is discussed in detail by Marianne McDonald, *Euripides in Cinema: the Heart Made Visible* (Philadelphia: Centrum, 1983), pp. 89-127.

11. Rudkin, Foreword, p. iii.

12. This is true throughout his career in Greek mythology: he abandons Ariadne and causes the death of his father Aegeus by forgetting to change his sails from black to white; he destroys Hippolytus with his curse; and in old stories, when he goes to the underworld, he is imprisoned there, as a punishment for trying to abduct its queen. The Athenians who made him their patron hero reinvented all these myths in order to sanitise him as a suitable national representative: see my *Theseus, Tragedy and the Athenian Empire* (Oxford: Oxford University Press, 1997).

13. *Hippolyta* by Manuel Fernandes, reviewed by Marianne McDonald in *Didaskalia*, an electronic journal of Greek tragedy in modern production, vol. 1.3, August 1994: http://didaskalia.berkeley.edu/.

14. I know of this production only through the website http://www.weeklywire.com/ww/07-13-98/slc_ae.html) and have not been able to locate a text of it or to read the version itself.

15. Lope de Vega's *El Castigo sin Venganza* or Zola's *Le Curée* are but two that are often cited in this connection. Brian Friel's *Living Quarters* is also structured around similar themes: see Marianne McDonald, 'Violent Words: Brian Friel's *Living Quarters: After Hippolytus*', *Arion* 6.1 (1998), pp. 35ff.

16. For a full account of her work on the myth, see *Hilda Doolittle* by Vincent Quinn (New York: Twayne, 1967), pp. 50-1, 104-11.

17. John Walsh, endnotes in *Hippolytus Temporizes: a Play in Three Acts* (Redding Ridge, CT: Black Swan Books, 1985), p. 141.

18. In Thomas Corneille's *Ariane* (1672), Phaedra is punished for running off with Theseus and abandoning Ariadne on Naxos by what happens to her with Hippolytus in Athens.

19. This kind of explanation of how things come to be is common in Greek tragedy – Artemis' promise of a cult to Hippolytus at the end of Euripides explains the existence of the cult to contemporary Athenians.

Guide to Further Reading

Translations

I have written for an audience that does not know Greek, but everyone knows Robert Frost's definition of poetry as that which gets lost in translation, and reading a translation of the *Hippolytus* will only hint at Euripides' subtlety, beauty and even, in places, his meaning. If this book inspires even one person to learn Greek – if it has, let me know! – I will be delighted. In the meantime, a number of reliable translations exist. David Grene's translation (Chicago: University of Chicago Press, 1942) is accurate, and makes some attempt to convey Euripides' poetry. Philip Vellacott's version (Harmondsworth: Penguin, 1974) is prosey and strangely omits Phaedra's crucial words on 'shame' at 385-7. The translation by Frederick Raphael and Kenneth McLeish (London: Methuen, 1997) is vigorous and modern, but sometimes deviates from a close rendition of the Greek, and renders the Greek expressions of distress '*oimoi*' and '*pheu*' phonetically as 'oee mooe' (309) and 'feoo feoo' (242), which I found distracting. James Morwood's translation (Oxford: Oxford University Press, 1998) includes an excellent introduction by Edith Hall, and is accurate, if unpoetic. *Euripides' Hippolytus: a Companion with Translation* (Bristol: Bristol Classical Press, 1986) by Gilbert and Sarah Lawall contains a useful introduction and handy notes keyed to the translation.

Texts, commentaries and parallel texts

Euripides Fabulae, vol. 1, ed. J. Diggle (Oxford: Clarendon Press, 1984). The standard text of the *Hippolytus* for those who read it in Greek.

Barrett, *Commentary*. W.S. Barrett, *Hippolytos: Edited with Introduction and Commentary* (Oxford: Clarendon Press, 1964). Unsurpassable in scholarship, but indigestible for beginners.

Richard Hamilton, *Euripides' Hippolytus* (Bryn Mawr, PA: Bryn Mawr

Commentaries, 1982) A basic undergraduate text and commentary which gives much more grammatical help than does Barrett.

Halleran, *Commentary*. M. Halleran, *Euripides' Hippolytus with Introduction, Translation and Commentary* (Warminster, England: Aris & Phillips, 1995). The best value for money, offering an excellent introduction, parallel text and a brief commentary.

David Kovacs, *Children of Heracles; Hippolytus; Andromache; Hecuba* (Cambridge, MA: Harvard University Press, 1995). A new and valuable text and translation.

General books and articles on Greek tragedy

Easterling, *Cambridge Companion*. P.E. Easterling, *Cambridge Companion to Greek Tragedy* (Cambridge: Cambridge University Press, 1997). A superb collection of essays on various aspects of Greek theatre.

Goldhill, *Reading Greek Tragedy*. S. Goldhill, *Reading Greek Tragedy* (Cambridge: Cambridge University Press, 1986). An important, theoretically sophisticated book on Greek tragedy.

Goldhill, 'The Great Dionysia'. S. Goldhill, 'The Great Dionysia and Civic Ideology', in J.J. Winkler and F.I. Zeitlin (editors), *Nothing to do with Dionysus?* (Princeton: Princeton University Press, 1990), pp. 97-129. A very important article on the social context of Athenian tragedy.

Gould, 'Tragedy in Performance'. John Gould, 'Tragedy in Performance', *Cambridge History of Classical Literature* (Cambridge, Cambridge University Press, 1982), pp. 263-80. Concise but detailed account of the practical aspects of Greek theatre.

Pickard-Cambridge, *Dramatic Festivals*. A. Pickard-Cambridge, *The Dramatic Festivals of Athens* (1st ed. Oxford 1953; 2nd ed. revised by J. Gould and D.M. Lewis reissued with new supplement (Oxford: Clarendon Press, 1988). Fundamental to all discussions of Greek tragic theatre.

Taplin, *Greek Tragedy*. O.P. Taplin, *Greek Tragedy in Action* (London: Methuen, 1978). A valuable insistence on the visual, as well as the textual aspects of tragedy.

General books and articles on Euripides

Conacher, *Euripidean Drama*. D.J. Conacher, *Euripidean Drama: Myth, Theme and Structure* (Toronto: University of Toronto Press, 1967). A good general introduction to Euripides.

Grube, *Drama*. G.M.A. Grube, *The Drama of Euripides* (New York: Barnes & Noble, 1961). A solid general study of Euripides.

Stevens, 'Euripides': P.T. Stevens, 'Euripides and the Athenians', *Jour-

Guide to Further Reading

nal of Hellenic Studies 76 (1956), pp. 87-94. A sensible article on Athenian attitudes to their controversial but admired playwright.

Books and articles on the *Hippolytus*

Cairns, *Aidôs*. D. Cairns, *Aidôs: The Psychology and Ethics of Honour and Shame in Ancient Greek Literature* (Oxford: Clarendon Press, 1993), pp. 322-40. A useful book on an important concept in the *Hippolytus*.

Dimock 'Virtue Rewarded'. G.E. Dimock, 'Virtue Rewarded', *Yale Classical Studies* 25 (1977), pp. 239-58. One of Hippolytus' most devoted admirers.

Dodds, '*Aidôs*'. E.R. Dodds, 'The *Aidôs* of Phaedra and the Meaning of the *Hippolytus*', *Classical Review* 39 (1925), pp. 102-4. A classic treatment of *aidôs* in the play.

Fitzgerald, 'Misconception'. G.J. Fitzgerald, 'Misconception, Hypocrisy, and the Structure of Euripides' *Hippolytus*', *Ramus* 2 (1973), pp. 20-40. Hostile to Phaedra and to divinely motivated explanations for the events.

Knox, '*Hippolytus*'. B.M.W. Knox, 'The *Hippolytus* of Euripides', originally published in *Yale Classical Studies* 13 (1952), pp. 3-31, reprinted in *Word and Action: Essays in the Ancient Theatre* (Baltimore, Johns Hopkins University Press), pp. 205-30. A classic article and excellent starting point for considering the main themes of the play.

Kovacs, 'Shame, Pleasure, Honor'. David Kovacs, 'Shame, Pleasure and Honour in Phaedra's Great Speech (E. *Hipp.* 375-87)', *American Journal of Philology* 101 (1981), pp. 287-303. A detailed but clear article on the difficulties of interpretation in Phaedra's great speech.

Kovacs, *Heroic Muse*: David Kovacs, *The Heroic Muse: Studies in the Hippolytus and Hecuba of Euripides* (Baltimore: Johns Hopkins University Press, 1987). A very important study of the play.

Lattimore, 'Euripides' Phaedra'. Richmond Lattimore, 'Euripides' Phaedra and Hippolytus' in Sanderson and Gopnik, pp. 283-96, reprinted from 'Phaedra and Hippolytus', *Arion* 1 (1962), pp. 5-18. Discusses the story pattern of the play and parallels.

Luschnig, *Time Holds the Mirror*. C.A.E. Luschnig, *Time Holds the Mirror: a Study of Knowledge in Euripides' Hippolytus* (Leiden & New York: E.J. Brill, 1988). A useful and intelligent study of the play.

Roisman, *Nothing is What it Seems*. H. Roisman, *Nothing is What it Seems* (Lanham, Md.: Rowman and Littlefield, 1999). A stimulating read, if just for disagreement.

Segal, 'Pentheus and Hippolytus'. Charles Segal, 'Pentheus and Hip-

144

polytus on the Couch and on the Grid: Psychoanalytic and Structuralist readings of Greek Tragedy', *Classical World* 72 (1978/9), pp.
129-48, reprinted in *Interpreting Greek Tragedy: Myth, Poetry, Text*
(Ithaca, NY: Cornell University Press, 1986), pp. 268-92. A good
introduction to structuralist and psychological readings of Greek
tragedy.

Strauss, *Fathers and Sons*. Barry Strauss, *Fathers and Sons in Athens:
Ideology and Society in the Era of the Peloponnesian War* (Princeton, NJ: Princeton University Press, 1993). A study of a topic of
importance in ancient Athens and in the *Hippolytus*.

Willink, 'Some Problems'. C. Willink, 'Some Problems of Text and
Interpretation in the Hippolytus', *Classical Quarterly* 18 (1968), pp.
11-43. Not easy, but important. Willink's interpretation differs
greatly from that taken by this book.

Winnington Ingram, 'Hippolytus', R.P. Winnington Ingram, 'Hippolytus: A Study in Causation', in *Euripide: sept exposés et
discussions* par J.C. Kamerbeek et al., Vandoeuvres-Genève, 4-9
août 1958 (Geneva: Fondation Hardt, 1960), pp. 171-97. A very
influential interpretation of the play.

Zeitlin, 'Power of Aphrodite'. Froma Zeitlin, 'The Power of Aphrodite:
Eros and the Boundaries of the Self in Hippolytus', pp. 52-111 in
Peter Burian (ed.), *Directions in Euripidean Criticism: a Collection
of Essays* (Durham, NC: Duke University Press, 1985). Not an easy
read, but an important article.

The Hippolytus myth after Euripides

Francis, *Métamorphoses*. Claude Francis, *Les métamorphoses de
Phèdre dans la littérature française* (Quebec: Editions du Pélican,
1967). A witty account of the Hippolytus and Phaedra tradition in
France.

Lucas, *Euripides and His Influence*. F.L. Lucas, *Euripides and His
Influence* (New York: Cooper Square Publishers, 1963). A useful
book on Euripides and later literature.

Michelini, *Euripides*. Ann Norris Michelini, *Euripides and the Tragic
Tradition* (Madison, Wis.: University of Wisconsin Press, 1987). A
helpful account of the history of Euripidean scholarship.

Sanderson and Gopnik: James Sanderson and Irwin Gopnik (editors),
Phaedra and Hippolytus – Myth and Dramatic Form (Boston:
Houghton Mifflin, 1966). A convenient anthology comprising
Euripides' *Hippolytus*, Seneca's *Phaedra*, Racine's *Phèdre*, Robin-
son Jeffers' *The Cretan Woman* and Eugene O'Neill's *Desire Under
the Elms*, with interpretative essays.

Women in the ancient world

Blundell, *Women*. Sue Blundell, *Women in Ancient Greece* (Cambridge, MA: Harvard University Press, 1994). Very readable detailed account of women in Greece.

Gould, 'Law, Custom and Myth'. John Gould, 'Law, Custom and Myth: Aspects of the Social Position of Women in Classical Athens', *Journal of Hellenic Studies* 100 (1980), pp. 38-59. An important article on women in Athens.

Just, *Women*: Roger Just, *Women in Athenian Law and Life* (London: Routledge, 1989). An excellent account written from an anthropological point of view.

The sophists

Guthrie, *The Sophists*. W.K.C. Guthrie, *The Sophists* (Cambridge: Cambridge University Press, 1981). The standard account of the sophists in Athens.

Bibliography

H. Avery, 'My Tongue Swore, But My Mind is Unsworn', *Transactions of the American Philological Association* 99 (1968), pp. 19-35.

S.A. Barlow, *The Imagery of Euripides: a Study in the Dramatic Use of Pictorial Language* (London: Methuen, 1971).

H.E. Barnes, *The Hippolytus of Drama and Myth* (Lincoln, NE: University of Nebraska Press, 1960).

W.S. Barrett, *Hippolytos*. Edited with introduction and commentary (Oxford: Clarendon Press, 1964).

E.M. Blaiklock, *The Male Characters of Euripides: a Study in Realism* (Wellington: New Zealand University Press, 1952).

J. Blomqvist, 'Human and Divine Action in Euripides' *Hippolytus*', *Hermes* 110 (1982), pp. 398-414.

S. Blundell, *Women in Ancient Greece* (Cambridge, MA: Harvard University Press, 1994).

G.W. Bond, 'A Chorus in Hippolytus: Manuscript Text versus Dramatic Realism', *Hermathena* 129 (1980), pp. 59-63.

P. Burian, 'Tragedy Adapted for Stages and Screens: the Renaissance to the Present', in Easterling, *Cambridge Companion*, pp. 228-83.

D. Cairns, *Aidôs: the Psychology and Ethics of Honour and Shame in Ancient Greek Literature* (Oxford: Clarendon Press, 1993).

D. Claus, 'Phaedra and the Socratic Paradox', *Yale Classical Studies* 22 (1972), pp. 223-38.

M. Coffey and R. Mayer (editors) *Seneca's Phaedra* (Cambridge: Cambridge University Press, 1990).

D. Cohen, 'Seclusion, Separation and the Status of Women', *Greece and Rome* 36 (1989), pp. 3-15.

C. Collard, *Euripides* (Oxford: Clarendon Press, 1981).

D.J. Conacher, *Euripidean Drama: Myth, Theme and Structure* (Toronto: University of Toronto Press, 1967).

E.M. Craik, '*Aidôs* in Euripides' *Hippolytos* 373-430: review and reinterpretation', *Journal of Hellenic Studies* 113 (1993), pp. 45-59.

———— 'Language of Sexuality and Sexual Inversion in Euripides' *Hippolytus*', *Acta Classica* 41 (1998), pp. 29-44.

147

Bibliography

J.N. Davidson, *Courtesans and Fishcakes: the Consuming Passions of Classical Athens* (London: HarperCollins, 1997).

G. Devereux, *The Character of the Euripidean Hippolytos: an Ethnopsychoanalytical Study* (Chico, CA: Scholars Press, 1985).

G.E. Dimock, 'Virtue Rewarded', *Yale Classical Studies* 25 (1977), pp. 239-258.

E.R. Dodds, 'The *Aidôs* of Phaedra and the Meaning of the *Hippolytus*', *Classical Review* 39 (1925), pp. 102-4.

—— 'Euripides the Irrationalist' in *The Ancient Concept of Progress and Other Essays in Greek Literature and Belief* (Oxford: Clarendon Press, 1973), pp. 78-91.

—— *Commentary on Euripides' Bacchae* (Oxford: Clarendon Press, 1960).

P.E. Easterling, *The Cambridge Companion to Greek Tragedy* (Cambridge: Cambridge University Press, 1997).

A.J. Festugière, *Personal Religion Among the Greeks* (Berkeley, CA: University of California, 1954).

G.J. Fitzgerald, 'Misconception, Hypocrisy, and the Structure of Euripides' *Hippolytus*', *Ramus* 2 (1973), pp. 20-40.

H. Flashar, *Inszenierung der Antike: Das Griechische Drama auf der Buhne der Neuzeit 1585-1990* (Munich: Beck, 1991).

M. Stadter Fox, *The Troubling Play of Gender: The Phaedra Dramas of Tsvetaeva, Yourcenar, and H.D.* (Selinsgrove, PA: Susquehanna University Press, 2001).

C. Francis, *Les métamorphoses de Phèdre dans la littérature française* (Quebec: Editions du Pélican, 1967).

B. Frischer, 'Concordia Discors and Characterisation in Euripides' Hippolytus', *Greek, Roman and Byzantine Studies* 11 (1970), pp. 85-100.

W.D. Furley, 'Phaidra's Pleasurable *Aidôs* (Eur. *Hipp.* 380-7)', *Classical Quarterly* n.s. 46 (1996), pp. 84-90.

J.C. Gibert, 'Euripides' Hippolytus Plays: Which Came First', *Classical Quarterly* 47 (1997), pp. 85-97.

J. Glen, 'The Fantasies of Phaedra: a Psychoanalytic Reading', *Classical World* 69 (1976), pp. 435-42.

B.E. Goff, *The Noose of Words: Readings of Desire, Violence, and Language in Euripides' Hippolytos* (Cambridge: Cambridge University Press, 1990).

S. Goldhill, *Reading Greek Tragedy* (Cambridge: Cambridge University Press, 1986).

—— 'The Great Dionysia and Civic Ideology', in J.J. Winkler and F.I. Zeitlin (editors), *Nothing to do with Dionysus?* (Princeton: Princeton University Press, 1990), pp. 97-129.

—— 'Representing Democracy: Women at the Great Dionysia', in *Ritual, Finance, Politics: Democratic Accounts Presented to David Lewis* (Oxford: Clarendon Press, 1994), pp. 347-69.

Bibliography

—— 'Civic Ideology and the Problem of Difference: the Politics of Aeschylean Tragedy, Once Again', *Journal of Hellenic Studies* 120 (2000), pp. 34-56.

J. Gould, 'Hiketeia', *Journal of Hellenic Studies* 93 (1973), pp. 74-103.

—— 'Dramatic Character and Human Intelligibility', in *Greek Tragedy, Proceedings of the Cambridge Philological Society* 33 (1978), pp. 43-67.

—— 'Law, Custom and Myth: Aspects of the Social Position of Women in Classical Athens', *Journal of Hellenic Studies* 100 (1980), pp. 38-59.

—— 'Tragedy in Performance', *Cambridge History of Classical Literature* (Cambridge, Cambridge University Press, 1982), pp. 263-80.

L.H.G. Greenwood, *Aspects of Euripidean Tragedy* (New York: Russell & Russell, 1953).

J. Gregory, *Euripides and the Instruction of the Athenians* (Ann Arbor: University of Michigan Press, 1991).

D. Grene, *The Complete Greek Tragedies*, vol. 5 (Chicago: University of Chicago Press, 1942).

G.M.A. Grube, *The Drama of Euripides* (New York: Barnes & Noble, 1961).

W.K.C. Guthrie, *The Sophists* (Cambridge: Cambridge University Press, 1981).

M.R. Halleran, *The Stagecraft in Euripides* (Totowa, NJ: Barnes & Noble, 1984).

—— *Euripides' Hippolytus with Introduction, Translation and Commentary* (Warminster, England: Aris & Phillips, 1995).

S. Halliwell, *Aristotle's Poetics* (London/Chapel Hill, NC: Duckworth/University of North Carolina Press, 1986).

R. Hamilton, *Euripides' Hippolytus* (Bryn Mawr, PA: Bryn Mawr Commentaries, 1982).

K. Hartigan, *Greek Tragedy on the American Stage: Ancient Drama in the Commercial Theatre 1882-1994* (Westport, CT: Greenwood Press, 1995).

M. Heath, *The Poetics of Greek Tragedy* (London: Duckworth, 1987).

J. Henderson, 'Women and the Athenian Dramatic Festivals', *Transactions of the American Philological Society* 121 (1991), pp. 133-47.

H. Herter, 'Theseus und Hippolytos', *Rheinisches Museum für Philologie* 90 (1940), pp. 273-92.

E. Howald, *Die Griechische Tragödie* (Munich: Oldenbourg, 1930).

T.H. Irwin, 'Euripides and Socrates', *Classical Philology* 78 (1983), pp. 183-97.

R. Just, *Women in Athenian Law and Life* (London: Routledge, 1989).

S. Kawashima, 'AIDOS and EUKLEIA: Another Interpretation of Phaedra's Long Speech in the *Hippolytus*', *Studi Italiani di Filologia e Cultura* 4 (1988), pp. 183-94.

Bibliography

G. Kerferd, *The Sophistic Movement* (Cambridge: Cambridge University Press, 1981).

B.M.W. Knox, 'The *Hippolytus* of Euripides', originally published in *Yale Classical Studies* 13 (1952), pp. 3-31, reprinted in *Word and Action: Essays in the Ancient Theatre* (Baltimore, Johns Hopkins University Press), pp. 205-30.

D. Kovacs, 'Shame, Pleasure and Honour in Phaedra's Great Speech (E. *Hipp.* 375-87)', *American Journal of Philology* 101 (1981), pp. 287-303.

―――― *The Heroic Muse: Studies in the Hippolytus and Hecuba of Euripides* (Baltimore: Johns Hopkins University Press, 1987).

―――― *Children of Heracles; Hippolytus; Andromache; Hecuba* (Cambridge, MA: Harvard University Press, 1995).

R. Lattimore, 'Euripides' Phaedra and Hippolytus', in Sanderson and Gopnik, pp. 283-96, reprinted from 'Phaedra and Hippolytus', *Arion* 1 (1962), pp. 5-18.

G. Lawall and S. Lawall, *Euripides' Hippolytus: A Companion with Translation* (Bristol: Bristol Classical Press, 1986).

M.R. Lefkowitz, ' "Impiety" and "Atheism" in Euripides' Dramas', *Classical Quarterly* 39 (1989), pp. 70-82.

M.A. Lloyd, *The Agon in Euripides* (Oxford: Clarendon Press, 1992).

H. Lloyd-Jones, 'Psychology and the Study of the Ancient World', pp. 152-89 in *Freud and the Humanities*, ed. P. Horden (London/New York: Duckworth/St Martin's Press, 1985).

F.L. Lucas, *Euripides and his Influence* (New York: Cooper Square Publishers, 1963).

W. Luppe, 'Die Hypothesis zum Ersten "Hippolytos" ', *Zeitschrift für Papyrologie und Epigraphik* 102 (1994), pp. 23-39.

C.A.E. Luschnig, *Time Holds the Mirror: a Study of Knowledge in Euripides' Hippolytus* (Leiden & New York: E.J. Brill, 1988).

B. Manuwald, 'Phaidras Tragischer Irrtum', *Rheinisches Museum für Philologie* 122 (1979), pp. 134-8.

M. McDonald, *Euripides in Cinema: the Heart Made Visible* (Philadelphia: Centrum, 1983).

―――― 'Violent Words: Brian Friel's Living Quarters: After Hippolytus', *Arion* 6.1 (1998).

R.E. Meagher, *Mortal Vision: the Wisdom of Euripides* (New York: St. Martin's Press, 1989).

G.S. Meltzer, 'The "Just Voice" as Paradigmatic Metaphor in Euripides' Hippolytus', *Helios* 23 (1996), pp. 173-90.

A.N. Michelini, *Euripides and the Tragic Tradition* (Madison, Wis.: University of Wisconsin Press, 1987).

S. Mills, *Theseus, Tragedy and the Athenian Empire* (Oxford: Oxford University Press, 1997).

R. Mitchell-Boyask, 'Euripides' *Hippolytus* and the Trials of Manhood',

Bibliography

in *Rites of Passage in Ancient Greece: Literature, Religion, Society*, ed. M. Padilla (London: Associated University Presses, 1999).

J. Morwood, *Euripides: Medea; Hippolytus; Electra; Helen* (Oxford: Oxford University Press, 1998).

Gilbert Murray, *Euripides and His Age* (Oxford: Oxford University Press, 1946).

August Nauck, *Tragicorum Graecorum Fragmenta*, 2nd edn. (Hildesheim: Olms, 1964).

G. Norwood, *Essays on Euripidean Drama* (Berkeley, CA: University of California Press, 1954).

M. Orban, 'Hippolyte: Palinodie ou revanche?' *Les Etudes Classiques* 49 (1981), pp. 3-17.

S. Østerud, 'Who sings the Monody 669-79 in Euripides' *Hippolytus?*', *Greek, Roman and Byzantine Studies* 11 (1970), pp. 307-20.

V. Quinn, *Hilda Doolittle* (New York: Twayne, 1967).

R. Parker, 'Gods Cruel and Kind: Tragic and Civic Theology', in C. Pelling, *Greek Tragedy and the Historian* (Oxford: Clarendon Press, 1997), pp. 143-61.

A. Pickard-Cambridge, *The Dramatic Festivals of Athens* (1st ed. Oxford 1953; 2nd ed. revised by J. Gould and D.M. Lewis and reissued with new supplement (Oxford: Clarendon Press, 1988).

N. Rabinowitz, *Anxiety Veiled: Euripides and the Traffic in Women* (Ithaca, NY: Cornell University Press, 1993).

A.V. Rankin, 'Euripides' Hippolytus: a Psychopathological Hero', *Arethusa* 7 (1974), pp. 71-94.

F. Raphael and K. McLeish, *Euripides: Six Plays* (London: Methuen, 1997).

K.J. Reckford, 'Phaedra, Hippolytus, Aphrodite', *Transactions of the American Philological Society* 103 (1972), pp. 405-32.

———— 'Phaedra and Pasiphae: the Pull Backward', *Transactions of the American Philological Society* 104 (1973), pp. 307-28.

R. Rehm, *Greek Tragic Theatre* (London: Routledge, 1992).

A. Rivier, *Essai sur le tragique d'Euripide*, 2nd ed. (Paris: Diffusion De Boccard, 1975).

H. Roisman, *Nothing is What it Seems* (Lanham, MD: Rowman and Littlefield, 1999).

J. Sanderson and I. Gopnik (editors), *Phaedra and Hippolytus – Myth and Dramatic Form* (Boston: Houghton Mifflin, 1966).

C.P. Segal, 'Shame and Purity in *Euripides*' Hippolytus', *Hermes* 98 (1970), pp. 278-99.

———— 'Pentheus and Hippolytus on the Couch and on the Grid: Psychoanalytic and Structuralist Readings of Greek Tragedy', *Classical World* 72 (1978/9), pp. 129-48, reprinted in *Interpreting Greek Tragedy: Myth, Poetry, Text* (Ithaca, NY: Cornell University Press, 1986), pp. 268-92.

Bibliography

————— *Euripides and the Poetics of Sorrow: Art, Gender, and Commemoration in Alcestis, Hippolytus, and Hecuba* (Durham, NC: Duke University Press, 1993).

————— 'The Tragedy of the Hippolytus: the Waters of Ocean and the Untouched Meadow', *Harvard Studies in Classical Philology* 70 (1965), pp. 117-69, reprinted in *Interpreting Greek Tragedy: Myth, Poetry, Text* (Ithaca, NY: Cornell University Press, 1986), pp. 166-209.

E. Segal, *Euripides: a Collection of Critical Essays* (Englewood Cliffs, N J: Prentice-Hall, 1968).

W.D. Smith, 'Staging in the Central Scene of the *Hippolytus*', *Transactions of the American Philological Association* 91 (1960), pp. 162-77.

B. Snell, *Scenes from Greek Drama* (Berkeley: University of California Press, 1964).

A.H. Sommerstein, 'Notes on Euripides' Hippolytus', *Bulletin of the Institute of Classical Studies* 35 (1988), pp. 23-41.

W.B. Stanford, 'The *Hippolytus* of Euripides', *Hermathena* 63 (1944), pp. 11-17.

P.T. Stevens, 'Euripides and the Athenians', *Journal of Hellenic Studies* 76 (1956), pp. 87-94.

B. Strauss, *Fathers and Sons in Athens: Ideology and Society in the Era of the Peloponnesian War* (Princeton, NJ: Princeton University Press, 1993).

O.P. Taplin, *Greek Tragedy in Action* (London: Methuen, 1978).

P. Vellacott, *Three Plays: Alcestis, Hippolytus, Iphigeneia in Tauris* (Harmondsworth: Penguin, 1974).

————— *Ironic Drama: a Study of Euripides' Method and Meaning* (Cambridge: Cambridge University Press, 1975).

A.W. Verrall, *Euripides the Rationalist: a Study in the History of Arts and Religion* (Cambridge: Cambridge University Press, 1895).

J. Michael Walton, *Greek Theatre Practice* (Westport, CT: Greenwood Press, 1980).

————— *Living Greek Theatre: a Handbook of Classical Performance and Modern Production* (Westport, CT: Greenwood Press, 1987).

E.F. Watling, *Seneca, Four Tragedies and Octavia* (Harmondsworth: Penguin, 1966).

T.B.L. Webster, *The Tragedies of Euripides* (London: Methuen, 1967).

B. Williams, *Shame and Necessity* (Berkeley, CA: University of California Press, 1993).

C. Willink, 'Some Problems of Text and Interpretation in the Hippolytus', *Classical Quarterly* 18 (1968), pp. 11-43.

P. Wilson, *The Athenian Institution of the Khoregia: the Chorus, the City and the Stage* (Cambridge, Cambridge University Press, 2000).

R.P. Winnington Ingram, 'Hippolytus: a Study in Causation', in *Euripide: sept exposés et discussions* par J.C. Kamerbeek et al.,

Bibliography

Vandoeuvres-Genève, 4-9 août 1958 (Geneva: Fondation Hardt, 1960), pp. 171-97.

Froma Zeitlin, 'The Power of Aphrodite: Eros and the Boundaries of the Self in Hippolytus', pp. 52-111 in Peter Burian (ed.), *Directions in Euripidean Criticism: a Collection of Essays* (Durham, NC: Duke University Press, 1985).

C. Zintzen, *Analytisches Hypomnema zu Senecas Phaedra* (Meisenheim am Glan: Hain, 1960).

Walter Zürcher, *Die Darstellung des Menschen im Drama des Euripides* (Basle: Reinhardt, 1947).

Glossary of Ancient and Technical Terms

Agôn. 'Contest' consisting of a monologue by one character on an issue central to the tragedy, answered by a second speech attempting a refutation of the first speaker's position. A dialogue between the two participants follows.

Aidôs, aidoumai. Meanings of these words include the English 'shame', 'self-restraint' and 'reverence'. Central to the concept is the idea of inhibition of impulses through considerations of morality or of others' opinions. Different characters in the *Hippolytus* have different ideas of its true nature.

Aretê. Excellence, whether moral, technical or other.

Chorêgos. Wealthy private citizen who paid for the expenses necessary to train a tragic chorus.

Dochmiacs. Tragic metre restricted to moments of high emotion. u– –u– is the basic dochmiac rhythm, but a large number of variations is possible.

Eisodoi or *parodoi*. Two paths on either side of the stage used as roads to and from the city in which the drama was set.

Ekkyklêma. Wheeled wooden platform, located inside the *skênê* building and rolled out of it when the playwright shows a scene taking place indoors.

Episode. Scene of a tragedy.

Exodos. The final scene in a tragedy following the last choral song.

Iambic trimeter. Metre used for speeches and dialogue. Each line is composed of three 'feet' consisting of two iambs, a metrical unit consisting of one short syllable followed by a long one. The first syllable of each foot can be long or short and variations within the line are possible, but the basic rhythmic pattern is x–u– x–u– x–u–.

Orchêstra. 'Dancing place.' Part of the stage where the chorus performed.

Parodos. Song sung by the chorus at their first entry early in the play.

Semnos, sebomai. Ranging in meaning from 'reverend' to 'arrogant' (someone who demands to be revered), the concept is explored in a series of word-plays that run through the play. See especially Chapter 4.

Skênê. Building on the stage which stood for any place entered by the characters in a tragedy.

Stasimon. Song sung by the chorus to separate the different scenes (episodes) of the tragedy from one another.

Sôphrosynê, sôphronein. Literally 'safe-mindedness', the word ranges from 'good sense' to 'self-control' to 'virtue'. It is often joined with *aidôs*, and like *aidôs*, what it truly consists of is the source of much speculation in the play.

Stichomythia. A kind of stylised conversation between actors who speak to one another in alternating lines. Often used to provide excitement in a tragedy by speeding up its dialogue.

Theologeion. Flat roof of the *skênê*, on which divine epiphanies could take place.

Chronology

Some adaptations not discussed in the text are included here.

End of 1st cent. BC: *Heroides* 4, Ovid (poem)
Early 50s AD: *Phaedra*, Seneca (drama)
1571: *Hippolyte*, Robert Garnier (drama)
1591: *Hippolyte: tragédie tournée de Sénèque*, Jean Yeuwain (drama)
1626: *Les Amours de Diane et Hypolite*, Puget de la Serre (narrative)
1634: *Hippolyte*, Guérin de la Pinelière (drama)
1646: *Hypolite ou le Garçon Insensible*, Gabriel Gilbert (drama)
1672: *Ariane*, Thomas Corneille (drama)
1675: *Hippolyte*, Mathieu Bidar (drama)
1677: *Phèdre*, Jacques Pradon (drama)
1677: *Phèdre*, Jean Racine (drama)
1707: *Phaedra and Hippolytus*, Edmund Smith (drama)
1733: *Hippolyte et Aricie*, Jean Rameau (opera)
1843: 'Artemis Prologises', Robert Browning (poem)
1866: 'Phaedra', A. Swinburne (poem)
1873: *Phèdre*, Jules Massenet (overture)
1891: *Hippolytos*, Ulrich von Wilamowitz-Moellendorf (German translation and notes)
1908: *Euripides*, translated into English rhyming verse, Gilbert Murray (translation)
1909: *Fedra*, Gabriele d'Annunzio (drama)
1924: *Desire Under the Elms*, Eugene O'Neill (drama)
1926: Music to d'Annunzio's *Fedra*, Arthur Honegger
1927: *Hippolytus Temporizes: a Play in Three Acts*, H.D. (drama)
1946: *Thesée*, André Gide (novel)
1950: *Phèdre*, Jean Cocteau, music by Georges Auric (ballet)
1951: *Beyond the Mountains*, Kenneth Rexroth (drama)
1954: *The Cretan Woman*, Robinson Jeffers (drama)
1958: *The King Must Die*, Mary Renault (novel)
1962: *The Bull from the Sea*, Mary Renault (novel)
1962: *Phaedra*, Jules Dassin (film)

Chronology

1964: *Commentary on the Hippolytus* by W.S. Barrett
1975: 'Phaedra', Benjamin Britten (cantata)
1980: *Hippolytus: A Version*, David Rudkin (drama)
1985: *Phaedra: A Novel of Ancient Athens*, June Rachuy Brindel (novel)
1994: *Hippolyta*, Manuel Fernandes (drama)
1995: *Ode to Phaedra*, George Roumanis (opera)
1998: *Hippolytus*, Steven Porter (drama)

Index

Index